Worship Frames

Worship Frames

How We Shape and Interpret
Our Experience of God

Deborah J. Kapp

THE
ALBAN
INSTITUTE

Herndon, Virginia
www.alban.org

The Alban Institute
2121 Cooperative Way, Suite 100
Herndon, VA 20171-5370

Unless otherwise noted, all Scripture quotations are from the New Revised Standard Version of the Bible, copyright © 1989, Division of Christian Education of the National Council of the Churches of Christ in the United States of America, and are used by permission.

For the Life That You Have Given, Words: Carl P. Daw, Jr., copyright © 1990 Hope Publishing Company, Carol Stream, IL 60188. All rights reserved. Used by permission. Reprinted under license #64422.

God Is Here!, Words: Fred Pratt Green, copyright © 1979 Hope Publishing Company, Carol Stream, IL 60188. All rights reserved. Used by permission. Reprinted under license #64422.

Cover design by Tobias Becker, Bird Box Design.

Library of Congress Cataloging-in-Publication Data

Kapp, Deborah J.
  Worship frames : how we shape and interpret our experience of God / Deborah J. Kapp ; foreword by John M. Buchanan.
     p. cm. — (Vital worship, healthy congregations)
  Includes bibliographical references.
  ISBN 978-1-56699-367-8
  1. Public worship. I. Title.

BV15.K37 2008
264—dc22
                                        2008023663

Contents

119799

Series Editor's Foreword

Healthy Congregations

Christianity is a "first-person plural" religion, where communal worship, service, fellowship, and learning are indispensable for grounding and forming individual faith. The strength of Christianity in North America depends on the presence of healthy, spiritually nourishing, well-functioning congregations. Congregations are the cradle of Christian faith, the communities in which children of all ages are supported, encouraged, and formed for lives of service. Congregations are the habitat in which the practices of the Christian life can flourish.

As living organisms, congregations are by definition in a constant state of change. Whether the changes are in membership, pastoral leadership, lay leadership, the needs of the community, or the broader culture, a crucial mark of healthy congregations is their ability to deal creatively and positively with change. The fast pace of change in contemporary culture, with its bias toward, not against, change only makes the challenge of negotiating change all the more pressing for congregations.

Vital Worship

At the center of many discussions about change in churches today is the topic of worship. This is not surprising, for worship is at the center of congregational life. To "go to church" means, for most members of congregations, "to go to worship." In *How Do*

We Worship? Mark Chaves begins his analysis with the simple assertion, "Worship is the most central and public activity engaged in by American religious congregations" (Alban Institute, 1999, p. 1). Worship styles are one of the most significant reasons that people choose to join a given congregation. Correspondingly, they are central to the identity of most congregations.

Worship is also central on a much deeper level. Worship is the locus of what several Christian traditions identify as the nourishing center of congregational life: preaching, common prayer, and the celebration of ordinances or sacraments. Significantly, what many traditions elevate to the status of "the means of grace" or even the "marks of the church" are essentially liturgical actions. Worship is central, most significantly, for theological reasons. Worship both reflects and shapes a community's faith. It expresses a congregation's view of God and enacts a congregation's relationship with God and each other.

We can identify several specific factors that contribute to spiritually vital worship and thereby strengthen congregational life.

- Congregations, and the leaders that serve them, need a shared vision for worship that is grounded in more than personal aesthetic tastes. This vision must draw on the deep theological resources of Scripture, the Christian tradition, and the unique history of the congregation.
- Congregational worship should be integrated with the whole life of the congregation. It can serve as the "source and summit" from which all the practices of the Christian life flow. Worship both reflects and shapes the life of the church in education, pastoral care, community service, fellowship, justice, hospitality, and every other aspect of church life.
- The best worship practices feature not only good worship "content," such as discerning sermons, honest prayers, creative artistic contributions, celebrative and meaningful rituals for baptism and the Lord's Supper. They also arise of out of good process, involving meaningful contributions from participants, thoughtful leadership, honest evaluation, and healthy communication among leaders.

Vital Worship, Healthy Congregations Series

The Vital Worship, Healthy Congregations Series is designed to reflect the kind of vibrant, creative energy and patient reflection that will promote worship that is both relevant and profound. It is designed to invite congregations to rediscover a common vision for worship, to sense how worship is related to all aspects of congregational life, and to imagine better ways of preparing both better "content" and better "process" related to the worship life of their own congregations.

It is important to note that strengthening congregational life through worship renewal is a delicate and challenging task precisely because of the uniqueness of each congregation. This book series is not designed to represent a single denomination, Christian tradition, or type of congregation. Nor is it designed to serve as arbiter of theological disputes about worship. Books in the series will note the significance of theological claims about worship, but they may, in fact, represent quite different theological visions from each other or from our work at the Calvin Institute of Christian Worship. That is, the series is designed to call attention to instructive examples of congregational life and to explore these examples in ways that allow readers in very different communities to compare and contrast these examples with their own practice. The models described in any given book may for some readers be instructive as examples to follow. For others, a given example may remind them of something they are already doing well or something they will choose not to follow because of theological commitments or community history.

Deborah Kapp's *Worship Frames: How We Shape and Interpret Our Experience of God* offers a compelling metaphor for thinking about one of worship's central conundrums, namely, how we are to handle the concrete, palpable elements of human speech, movement, and singing, given that they become in worship occasions for nothing less than a divine-human encounter through the work of the Holy Spirit. Worship leaders offer words and actions that inevitably focus the attention, stimulate the imagination, shape the perceptions, and form the interactions of worshipers in one way or another. But this can be done either in a way that distracts from worship or in a way that helps worshipers pray the words of Psalm 63, "I have looked upon you in the sanctuary, beholding your power and glory." In worship, as with looking at a painting in a fine museum, our capacity to perceive a luminous power and beauty depends, in part, on having a suitable frame to shape our perceptions.

By promoting encounters with instructive examples from various parts of the body of Christ, we pray that these volumes will help leaders make good judgments about worship in their congregations and that, by the power of God's Spirit, these congregations will flourish.

John D. Witvliet
Calvin Institute of Christian Worship

Foreword

In the midst of a conversation about public worship that sometimes so escalates in intensity as to be called a "war," Deborah Kapp has written a thoughtful and helpful book. She has chosen fascinating anecdotal material to buttress her argument, which is solidly grounded in scholarship. And she has gently urged the combatants in the current worship wars to practice a ceasefire long enough to listen to one another and to learn from the valid arguments each makes. That is no small aspiration, and it holds the possibility of a creative peace in an arena of religious life that ought to be unifying people of faith rather than dividing them.

The truth is that the church, particularly that part of the church described as "mainline" or "mainstream," has a problem, and how it chooses to worship is just one expression of the larger dilemma in which we find ourselves. The problem is that a seismic cultural shift has occurred and is still in process, and our very best thinkers and scholars are struggling to understand it, name it, and describe it for us. There are many ways to define it. One way is ecclesiastically: the old accommodation between church and state, faith and culture, in Western Europe and North America is disappearing. Canadian theologian Douglas John Hall calls it the End of Christendom.[1] The numbers of people attending public worship in Western Europe continue to decline: not very long ago 98 percent of the Dutch people attended church regularly; today less than 10 percent attend. Similar statistics characterize church attendance in Great Britain, France, and Germany.

We are talking about postmodernism and its effects on the churches. For one thing, the culture no longer knows our vocabulary or our stories. Once when I referred to David's affair with Bathsheba in a sermon, I was surprised to discover the number of people who didn't know who David was. "Who was that David guy anyhow?" one of them asked.

In addition, the Christian, or Judeo-Christian, consensus is gone. The culture no longer knows the story. What the culture most knows is a narrative espoused and relentlessly marketed by the media, particularly television. Children in America watch an average of four and a half hours of television per day. Author and environmentalist Bill McKibben studied all the programs offered on television in a single twenty-four-hour period—twenty-four hundred hours of videotapes—and concluded that the singular message in sitcoms, game shows, talk shows, and commercials was "You are the most important thing on the face of the earth. Your immediate desires are all that count. Do it your way. This Bud's for you."[2]

In that context, planners of a countercultural activity such as public worship must be wise, discerning, creative, and faithful.

Presbyterian pastor and popular author Eugene Peterson says that traditional churches are "keepers of memory." For many of us, who we are, how we view the world, and what we believe were shaped by our early experience of public worship. The familiar, stately rhythm of traditional hymns, the aesthetic represented by stained-glass windows, Gothic architecture, and pictures of Jesus continue to resonate in memory and shape our faith. I can recall with precision what the church in which I worshiped as a child looked like. I can recall the feel of the pew cushions, the slightly musty odor, the sun streaming through the stained-glass window of Jesus praying in the Garden of Gethsemane. I spent a lot of time looking at that window, wondering at how young Jesus looked, so seemingly unconcerned with what was happening around him— you could see the vague shapes of Peter and his friends sleeping in the background—and at how clean his white robe was. I can recall Mary Wertz playing the organ up in the loft, as I sang with my parents "Holy, Holy, Holy," "For the Beauty of the Earth," and "This Is My Father's World." I can recall the people who sat around us—my Uncle Charles and Aunt Helen always on the aisle, the

Crawfords immediately in front of us. I remember staring at Mrs. Crawford's fabulous fox fur, which she wore wrapped around her shoulders. The fox head, with glass eyes, was directly in front of me, and that fox and I spent many an hour staring at each other. I recall mints from Mother's purse, and Dad's railroad watch, which he took from his vest pocket and wound, a little too ceremoniously, when he decided that the preacher had gone on too long. I recall the small door in the chancel through which the robed minister emerged—from what I thought must be a mysterious holy of holies—and I recall watching him bow his head and put his head in his hands to pray during the prelude, an act of impressive piety. I recall the elders on Communion Sunday—when elders were elderly men with white hair—walking solemnly and reverently to the first pew, to sit around the table. I recall the soprano soloist, with a vibrato at least a major third in breadth, who recruited her husband, the county coroner, a tenor with a big vibrato to match his wife's. When my Dad told me what the tenor did for a living, I could never stop thinking of that every time I saw him, especially on Christmas Eve, when he and his soprano wife knocked me out with a powerful "O Holy Night."[3] Much of who I am and what I believe was put in place, or at least framed, by that experience of worship.

Deborah Kapp is helpful in observing that the formative experiences will not be there for more and more people, nor will there be a memory. Kapp helped me finally to understand that although singing "Holy, Holy, Holy," with its stately rhythm and predictable, solid four-part harmony, and its gloriously eschatological imagery from the Book of Revelation, evokes sacred memory and is emotionally satisfying to me, it simply sounds peculiar, boring, dirgelike, and at times bizarre to a postmodern young adult who wanders into church some Sunday morning:

> Casting down their golden crowns around the glassy sea;
> Cherubim and seraphim falling down before Thee . . .

The great challenge is to understand the culturally endorsed narcissism of postmodernism and at the same time to hold on to the unique notion that worship is not a consumer product. In fact worship, traditional or contemporary, meditative or loud and noisy, is not "for" the worshipers but "for" God. World religion scholar Huston Smith observes that religion that focuses on the physical well-being and emotional satisfaction of the adherent turns the church into a service station/health club: "the opposite of religion's role which is to decenter the ego, not pander to its desires."[4]

Søren Kierkegaard said that a long time ago. People come to worship as if they were attending the theater, as an audience to enjoy a performance presented by the cast: preacher, choir, and organist. God, in this popular misconception, is the prompter, standing offstage, occasionally helping the performers with their lines. Whether worship works depends on the performance and on whether the audience has a good time. Theater is the correct context, Kierkegaard said. But God is the audience; the people in the congregation are the actors; the clergy and musicians are the prompters helping the worshipers worship. The analogy is still relevant. Mrs. Smith describes what she is doing on Sunday morning as "going to hear Reverend Adams"; Mr. Jones's morning is ruined because the minister and organist chose unfamiliar hymns; Ms. Brown announces that she's changing churches because she doesn't "get anything out of worship." Worship planners, whatever the particular style, need the Kierkegaardian reminder that the activity is supposed to encourage people to think about something other than themselves for an hour or so.

When he chose contemporary German drinking songs for hymn tunes, Martin Luther was said to have quipped that the devil doesn't have a monopoly on good music. It's a lesson those of us in the traditional church need to learn again. In fact, I think we need to reframe the conversation/argument/war. It should not be "traditional vs. contemporary," "pipe organ vs. praise band," "hymnals vs. pull-down screen." It is, or ought to be, "boring vs. interesting," "lifeless vs. energetic." I'm not at all convinced that traditional worship, by its very nature, is a boring, uninteresting activity. It often is, but it does not have to be. Nor is contemporary worship, by its very nature, interesting and lively. A pipe organ played by an energetic and creative musician is gloriously irresistible. A pipe organ played by an unimaginative organist is boring, but so is an acoustic guitar played by a boring guitarist.

Marva Dawn, who thinks and writes helpfully about liturgy, coined a useful phrase about some worship: "dumbed down." That is the culprit, whether contemporary or traditional: dumbed-down, simplistic, repetitive, unimaginative. Combine a dumbed-down liturgy with postmodern narcissism, and the result is not only boring but also misdirected, whether the congregation is singing a repetitive praise chorus or a syrupy, ever-popular, nineteenth-century hymn about walking alone in the garden with Jesus while the dew is on the roses.

Deborah Kapp provides new insights into the most visible characteristic of religion, how it invites its adherents to worship. Framing worship, the brackets of worship are helpful rubrics by which to understand why we worship as we do and why it is such a deeply emotional and powerful experience, however we express it. And the questions at the end of each chapter transform her scholarship into a practical workbook for those who plan and carry out worship and for those who want to understand it better.

This good book comes along at just the right time. Postmodernism has washed away the world with which I am familiar. I have to learn a new vocabulary, a new geography, a newly globalized politics. Part of what is in the very air out there is a longing for certainty. And religion—traditional and contemporary—as it invites people to worship, has an important and precious proposal, namely, a God whose goodness transcends everything that is happening in the world, yet who is deeply present in it; a God whose goodness is in all of life, but who loves each one of us as if there were only one of us to love; a God who lives in unknowing mystery and yet who comes as close as human love, human birth, a human life.

That is our job: to treasure the good news, and to create opportunities for people to know it, experience it, celebrate it, and thank God for the goodness of it; in worship to join a chorus of praise and gratitude that has been going on before we joined it for a while, and will go on after us, forever.

John M. Buchanan
Pastor, Fourth Presbyterian Church of Chicago
Editor/Publisher, *The Christian Century*

Preface

Worship is a congregation's most important practice. Here a congregation and its members encounter God's gracious presence and come face to face with the frailty, goodness, and potential of their humanity. Here they are comforted, corrected, forgiven, healed, challenged, and sometimes even disturbed by the divine and one another. Here congregations and people are morally formed, and from here they are sent by God into the world. Worship is important. Through the action of the Spirit it enlivens congregations and believers.

Because of its centrality to religious life, worship demands our attention and effort. Worship, in fact, results from the synergistic work of all its participants—God, worshipers, and leaders. Worship would be empty without God's active presence hearing, speaking, and inspiring our action. The mysterious and uncontrollable work of the Spirit is at the heart of all genuine worship. Yet at the same time, worshipers and leaders work hard to worship. People join the gathering and contribute their song, speech, silence, prayers, hearts, minds, and commitment. Leaders pray and prepare, select and arrange particular resources to enhance worship, and guide its flow.

This book uses a sociological perspective to examine the worship work that people do. The seeds of the book were planted several years ago, when I had the privilege of conducting a study that focused on congregational worship and mainline Protestant worship wars. I conducted research in three Presbyterian churches outside Chicago. Among them, the churches had four services weekly:

two traditional, one contemporary, and one blended (mostly contemporary).[1] For eight months I attended worship, conducted interviews, analyzed worship bulletins, studied congregational and neighborhood histories, and enjoyed the lives of the three churches. Unless otherwise noted, the quotes from worshipers and leaders and many of the examples of worship that appear in this book are drawn from this research. Other congregational studies, research and reading about leadership and worship, discussions with doctor of ministry students about their work, observations of worship in other congregations, and my own pastoral experience have given me insights, too, which will be evident in other observations and illustrations.

As I conducted my study, I did not have theological research questions. Rather, I was interested in trying to understand better the social and human dynamics of the worship wars that I heard ministers talk about so frequently. What is so different about worship styles, besides what might appear on the surface? What logics are at work in varying styles? And so what? What difference does a worship style make to a congregation? I was familiar with many discussions about questions like these in religious contexts, but I wanted to know what a sociological analysis might add to the discussion.

I learned more than I anticipated. I gained new insights into the worship wars, but I learned even more about worship itself and the work it involves. My respect grew for people in the pews, the wisdom and effort they bring to worship. My understanding of the structure and movement of worship expanded with new perspectives. I unmasked some of my past failings as a worship leader.

When I finished my work, I wanted to tell other people about what I'd learned. But it wasn't sociologists to whom I wanted to speak—it was ministers, church musicians, and other church members who make decisions about worship in their churches. I have, therefore, written this book to share my insights with congregations and worship leaders. I hope that readers will benefit from this book in several ways: gain added perspectives from which to analyze and design worship, deepen perceptions about the role that worship plays in forming church community and defining a congregation's public presence, and entertain ideas about how to strengthen worship, should they wish to do so in their congregation.

Frame analysis is the sociological theory that primarily informs this book, because it is the theory from which I learned the most. In my initial study, frame analysis opened my eyes to dynamics in worship that I had not noticed before, and it was this theory that best helped me understand differences in worship styles. Since then the concept of frame has also assisted me to design worship with more intentionality.

What is frame analysis? Briefly, a frame is an interpretive scheme or idea that helps people locate, understand, and identify their experience; and frame analysis is the study of frames and how they work.[2] Many congregational leaders are familiar with the concept of framing, because they have encountered it in discussions about church leadership or organizational management. My discussion here demonstrates how an understanding of frames can be applied to the practice of worship, too.

This book, then, is for congregations and their leaders. I hope it will provide ample content for group study and conversation, and will stimulate ministers, musicians, and other leaders as they consider the structures, dynamics, and leadership of worship. Although the book is solidly grounded in sociological analysis, it will undoubtedly—because it engages such a significant dimension of religious life, worship—raise theological issues and questions. I encourage readers to pursue these in small-group discussions and personal reflection.

Worship Frames

I engage four issues about framing and worship in this book: (1) definitions, (2) the capacity of frames to set boundaries and involve people in the action and ethos of worship, (3) the role frames can play in shaping a congregation's life and mission, and (4) the prickly issue of frames and change. I begin with a basic question: what is a frame? That's an important question, especially since scholars answer it in a number of different ways. So that readers

can tease apart my approach from that of others, I start chapter
1 with a discussion of four divergent ways that people define the
concept of frame. I also make clear which of those approaches I
use in this book.

In chapters 2 and 3 I move to a discussion of worship structures. Here I give particular attention to how worship frames set
the stage for worship, establish boundaries, orient people to worship's ethos and theology, and help worshipers to concentrate. I
also elaborate on why worshipers' concentration is important to
consider: the fact that worshipers pay attention in worship is not
as simple as it might seem to be.

With chapters 4 and 5 I shift to a discussion of the congregation as a whole, and explore how worship frames shape community in a congregation. Through an examination of worship
structures and discursive frames used in preaching, I illustrate how
frames can both shape belonging and articulate a congregation's
vocation.

I extend the discussion about frames and community in chapters 6 and 7, and raise the question of worship and change. How
can worship frames shape and interpret changes in a congregation's vocation? What steps might a congregation take, should it
want to strengthen its worship frames? What potential effect does
a frame change have?

Discussion questions at the ends of the chapters will aid readers who wish to use the book to think more intentionally about
worship.

Acknowledgments

I was surrounded by a great cloud of witnesses as I developed this
book, and I am grateful to every single one of them.

My dissertation was written with the help of several hundred people. The members of St. Luke Presbyterian Church and
First Presbyterian Church, both in Downers Grove, Illinois; and
Southminster Presbyterian Church, Arlington Heights, Illinois;
and their respective pastors, Howard Milkman, David Bianchin,
and Stephen Pierce, welcomed me into their midst with generous

hospitality. My committee—Fred Kniss, Marilyn Krogh, and the late Peter Whalley—prodded, directed, encouraged, and graced the study on which this book is based. Andrea Bertotti-Mertoyer, Paula Dempsey, Rebecca Burwell, and other classmates ran side by side. Morgan Simmons, beloved colleague, served as dissertation coach.

Several people read the dissertation or an earlier draft of this book and offered wise, generous counsel about publication: Bill McKinney, Carl Dudley, Alice Evans, Christine Vogel, John Burkhart, Lucy Hogan, Emily Brink, and John Witvliet. I am particularly grateful to Emily and John for their willingness to shepherd the book toward publication.

As I developed the final draft, many others offered helpful suggestions. My colleagues at McCormick Theological Seminary saw an earlier draft of chapters 4 and 5 and gave insightful critiques. Ideas for improvement came from people at the Calvin Institute of Christian Worship. But the most help came from Beth Gaede, who edited this book with patience, perspicacity, and good humor. Her sharp insights and appropriate questions helped me to focus and tighten my discussion. I hope I am a smarter writer as a result.

Generous support from three institutions also furthered this work. A grant from the Louisville Institute underwrote the costs of dissertation research. Sabbatical time granted me by McCormick Seminary provided mental space as well as fiscal and emotional support, and my colleagues cheered me along the way. A fellowship grant from the Cathedral College of Preachers provided much-needed space for restoration and creativity, as I wrote the final draft of this book.

My family and friends have sustained me through the highs and lows of graduate study, book writing, and publication. Tony, Geoffrey, Peter, Bobbi, Linda, Heidi, Jim, and Dean all deserve stars in their crowns—at the very least. Especially Tony, to whom this book is dedicated.

My deep thanks to you all.

CHAPTER 1

Frames

We were greeted warmly and handed bulletins when we walked into the sanctuary at Trinity United Church of Christ in Chicago. The church was beginning to fill, and all around us were church members and visitors in colorful African clothing. The church was bustling. People said hello to us and hailed their friends. About fifteen minutes before the worship service was scheduled to begin, a man came to the chancel, picked up a microphone, welcomed us, and invited us to stand. He began to sing, and we followed suit. Soon we were clapping along with the praise music in which he had invited us to join. Before we knew it the church was full, the clapping and drums and other instruments were lively, and music and energy filled the air. We realized that, without fanfare, a formal procession had begun, as a large choir with dozens of members in African dress came into the church and its members took their places in the choir loft that rose at the back of the chancel. Along with the choir came clergy and lay leaders who took seats in front of the choir. They, too, wore African dress. We sang and sang and sang.

We were framed.

At Lake View Presbyterian Church in Chicago we had an equally warm greeting from ushers and other worshipers as we arrived. We took our seats in the refurbished, 100-year-old sanctuary and sat quietly while we read the announcements that were projected on the wall behind the pulpit. The announcements scrolled by two or three times, telling us of the upcoming Gay Pride Parade, the summer worship schedule, and new adult-education classes. Shortly before worship began, a pianist played a prelude and the worship leaders entered. The pastor, who wore a robe, welcomed us to worship and led a call to worship, and the congregation joined in an opening hymn, followed by a prayer for peace. The pastor then invited people to share aloud their expressions of thanks. With what sense of gratitude did we come to worship that morning? She invited us to speak it.

We were framed.

At Willow Creek Community Church, a well-known megachurch in South Barrington, Illinois, we were also welcomed warmly as we walked in the front door, and our greeter volunteered to answer our questions or to guide us to a particular part of the church. We had arrived early, so there was time to look around. Some of us spent time at the food court or the bookstore. Others of us walked around and picked up literature or skimmed information at the computer kiosks in the lobby. We were all impressed with the friendliness of the people, the size and magnificence of the building, and the availability of support for worshipers. Before worship began, we made our way into the auditorium, where ushers gave us a printed sheet with announcements of church events, and we found our seats. The stage commanded our attention; it was professionally lit, and on it we could see band instruments and microphones. On either side of the stage huge projection screens depicted abstract images that coordinated with the background music that was playing. Right on schedule the band came on stage and began to play, a singer greeted us, and the praise-and-worship music began. We stood and joined in; as appropriate we sang, watched, and listened.

We were framed.[1]

All around the world, in all sorts of spaces and places and times and situations, Christian churches gather their members and friends for worship. People come together at a particular time and place; they join together in worship practices, some distinct to the community and others used by many churches; and they usher themselves into a shared awareness of divine presence. As they gather for worship, people are, in a word, framed.

This book examines the concept of frame, an idea used in a number of academic disciplines, as it might apply to corporate worship. As we shall see, frame is a robust concept that can be used in many ways, and several of these are useful in thinking about how worship is constructed, its impact on congregations and communities, and how congregations might approach change in worship structures.

Four Ways of Talking about Frame

As I noted earlier, a frame is a scheme or idea that helps people interpret their experience.[2] A frame enables its users to make sense of what is happening to them and to the world around them. It orients people and helps them know what they are doing (or are supposed to do) and who they are in relation to that activity.

"Frame" can be used as both a noun and a verb. When used as a verb, it refers to the capacity that human beings have to construct frames. Ronald Heifetz, for example, in his writings about leadership, has noted that leaders have the power to "frame" issues. By this he means that leaders have the social space, social capital, and visibility they need to define values and issues in ways that their followers can understand and to which they can respond appropriately.[3] Sometimes scholars take this idea one step further and speak of leaders' power to "reframe," to change and modify the original frames that shape people.[4]

Frame is such a supple concept that it is used effectively—but differently—by scholars in various disciplines. In what follows I identify and describe four distinct yet overlapping ways that people use the concept of frame. I do this so that we can see the lay of the framing landscape, because I have learned through difficult experience that it is easy to confuse the approaches. When that occurs, I cannot use any of them effectively. We can avoid confusion later by untangling some of the nuances of this concept now.

Frames as Boundaries

Remember the children's TV show, *Mr. Rogers' Neighborhood*? The show opened as Mr. Rogers appeared on the TV screen, sang his theme song, and invited the viewer to be his neighbor. While he was singing, he came through a door as if he were entering the front door of his home, took off his sport coat and put on a sweater, and changed from loafers into tennis shoes. He moved slowly and deliberately, and he addressed children as he talked about what would be happening on that episode. When the show concluded, he did all these things in reverse. He changed back into loafers and sport coat, sang another song, and walked out the door. Children watching knew exactly when the show started and when it was over. Mr. Rogers' songs, clothing changes, and use of the door signaled clear boundaries between the world outside his front door and the world inside his TV house.

In the middle of the show there was another sort of entrance and exit. The neighborhood trolley drove through a tunnel and entered the land of make-believe. There puppets acted out a story that had meaning for children's lives, sometimes with the help of Mr. Rogers' interpretation. When make-believe time was over, the trolley drove back through the tunnel into Mr. Rogers' living room. Children viewing the show understood when make-believe time began and ended. The show used the movement of the trolley to set clear boundaries between make-believe and real life.

The sociologist Erving Goffman discusses such boundary-drawing activity by using the concept of frame. Goffman defines a frame as an interpretive scheme or idea that helps people to understand and define their experience in ways that they find meaningful. A frame helps people to concentrate and focus. By lending coherence and meaning to an experience, a frame allows people to engage it in significant ways.

The frames used by Mr. Rogers helped children understand that they were spending special time with him in his neighborhood, and that some of that time was devoted to playing make-believe. His viewers knew that during the half-hour they spent with Mr. Rogers they left their own neighborhoods and were safe as they shared his. They also knew that when the half-hour was over they came back home.

The opening and closing frames that Mr. Rogers used were made up of several distinct things joined together—entrance/exit, changes of clothing, and songs. Goffman argues that sometimes frames are constructed in just this way: bundling together a group of conventionalized boundary markers that he calls "brackets." A simple example of a bracket is the sounding of a gavel to signify the beginning or adjournment of a meeting; the gavel's sound identifies the temporal boundaries of the meeting. Another example of bracketing is the series of markers that surround theatrical events in the West: the dimming of lights, orchestral music, and the curtain rising indicate that the play is about to begin; and when the play is finished, applause for the cast, falling curtain, closing music, and brightening of lights conclude it.[5] Sporting events have boundary markers, too, like the entrances and exits of teams and coaches, the singing of the national anthem at the beginning, and the sounding of whistles or horns to signal when the games start and conclude. By establishing strong boundaries to an activity, brackets signal what is to come or what has occurred; they tell us, "This is a meeting," or "You've been to the theater." Frame brackets also define the nature of frame action, including its degree of formality; they tell us, "It's time to be quiet because the meeting has started," or "Cheer loudly because your football team has just run onto the field." Goffman argues that the opening brackets of a frame are of particular importance, because they establish the action by setting the stage for what is to follow.[6]

Other scholars build on Goffman's work, take up more aspects of his argument, and talk about framing in other ways. At least three additional approaches to frame analysis have developed as a result.

Frames as Discourse

Some scholars point to the ways people use language to make and manage frames that are mental models, which evoke particular values or worldviews. These scholars argue that frames can be constructed through discourse. A funeral I attended about thirty years ago provides an apt illustration of this kind of frame.

The funeral celebrated the life of Mr. Logan, a middle-aged man who had been murdered in the course of an armed robbery in which he was an innocent bystander. He was the son of the retired sexton of the church where I was serving, and his father was devastated with grief. At the funeral the presiding minister delivered one of the most memorable sermons I have ever heard. His text was "Am I my brother's keeper?" (Gen. 4:9). The sermon was a magnificent expression of moral and religious outrage over the death of another human being. I remember the power and dignity that emanated from the pulpit that day.

In his sermon, the minister could have framed Mr. Logan's death differently. He could have made the father's grief the center-piece of the sermon, or he could have focused on the sadness of a life cut off prematurely. Neither of those choices would have been inappropriate, but instead the minister took another approach. He brought us face to face with God's grief and outrage over this death. "What have you done? Listen; your brother's blood is cry-ing out to me from the ground!" (Gen. 4:10). He challenged us all with an awareness of our shared moral responsibility for one an-other and for life, and reframed our understanding of the murder and its consequences. No longer was this man's death understood in the context of private grief and loss within a single family circle; now it was framed in a public and divine context, and it included all of us. "Am I my brother's keeper?" I surely am. And so are you.

This story illustrates the way that some people talk about fram-ing. George Lakoff, a prominent scholar of cognitive science and linguistics, works extensively with the idea of frame in his analyses of political speech. From his perspective, a frame is a mental con-struct that expresses shared values and shapes our understanding and approach to the world.[7] A mental frame normally exists at an unconscious level, and it is expressed with metaphors, or single words or phrases that evoke a larger worldview.[8] For example, think about the different sets of values that are evoked by two sim-ple phrases: "inheritance tax" and "death tax." Or think about the worldviews, feelings, and memories that are evoked when some-body talks about "marriage" or "family."[9] In themselves, these words or phrases might not be particularly descriptive, but they call to mind mental constructs—frames—that speak volumes.

Some social-movement scholars have also recognized the im-portance of framing as discourse, although they focus less on the use of metaphors and symbols and a discussion of values than do scholars like Lakoff. In studies of social movements, scholars demonstrate how leaders create movement frames with language and symbolic actions, and use the frames to construct meanings, which they then draw upon as they diagnose situations and prescribe responses, motivate actors, interpret a movement's goals to the public, demobilize opponents by confronting or undermining their arguments, and contribute to the effectiveness of a movement. Social-movement scholars also illustrate how dynamic frames can be, as they change during the ups and downs of a social movement.[10]

A good example of a social movement frame is the "pro-life" frame that the anti-abortion movement employs. By constructing a meaning for their efforts that focuses on the life of the unborn, movement leaders are able to energize their constituents around their commitment to life, direct members' energies toward saving the unborn, clarify the movement's position to the media, undermine the arguments about rights and privacy used by the women's movement to support access to abortion, and thus demobilize opponents. "Pro-life" grabs people with its expressive and interpretive force; for many people it is a much more compelling frame than is "pro-choice" or "a private decision between a woman and her physician." Built with language and symbolic actions, it is an extremely effective discursive frame that declares the movement's values, interprets its work, and motivates its adherents.

It is the discursive idea of framing on which Ronald Heifetz draws when he discusses the power that leaders have to frame debates, issues, and situations. Heifetz uses the example of Mohandas K. Gandhi, who appropriated and recast some of the deepest values of British culture to justify the Indian struggle to end British colonial rule. Martin Luther King, Jr., used a similar strategy in his "I have a dream" speech, when he drew on American values of equality, freedom, and hard work to support and explain the goals of the civil rights movement.[11] Both Gandhi and King were masters of framing and reframing.

The funeral sermon discussed above employed a discursive frame. The minister used biblical texts and a sermon—language— to evoke a particular set of values. The minister could have used a text such as "Blessed are those who mourn, for they will be comforted" (Matt. 5:4), a text that evokes Christian values of empathy, hope, and trust in God. He chose instead to use a text and preach a sermon that evoked Christian values of solidarity, social responsibility, and moral outrage. Both sets of values run deep in the Christian tradition, and the minister chose the value set that he deemed most appropriate for that situation. With his language and focus on a particular text, he framed the funeral and our worship around one set of values rather than another.

Frames as Problem Definitions and Resolutions

A third approach to frame analysis is to use the concept to think about how people define problems and propose resolutions for them. A frame in this sense is a way of interpreting a particular situation. Like conceptualizing frames as discourse, this approach relies on rhetoric and ways of talking about situations. It is, however, used to focus specifically on the challenges of diagnosing circumstances and prescribing solutions.

To illustrate this approach, think about this Sunday morning scene, which occurs almost every year in the church nursery: a young mother drops off her child in the nursery for the first time, and the child cries. The mother feels terrible. She tries to comfort the child; after a few minutes, she departs and goes to church. The next week the mother and child are back, and the child again cries; the mother once more stays with the child, but this time she remains a bit longer. The same thing happens the next Sunday. As the weeks drag on, the mother begins to question whether she should bother with church at all, since she spends more and more time in the nursery and misses an increasing proportion of the worship service. Finally, a nursery volunteer persuades the mother to do something different—to leave the nursery quickly, while the child is still crying. Sure enough, when the mother returns after church, the nursery volunteer tells her that the child ceased crying almost immediately after she left. What happened here? In a word, the nursery volunteer "reframed" the situation for the mother.

The concept of frame can be applied to situations like this— situations that seem to perpetuate themselves no matter how diligently people try to change them. The mother defines the problem as the child's discomfort with being in the nursery, and she prescribes maternal comfort as the solution. When a little comfort does not seem to work, the mother offers more—and more and more. Her solution to the problem still doesn't work. In fact, the more that maternal comfort is offered, the worse everything gets. The mother's solution fails repeatedly.

The nursery volunteer recognizes this cycle of problem definition and failed solution, and she defines the situation with a different frame. She pinpoints the failed solution as the problem. For her the issue is not that the child cries but rather that the mother perpetuates the crying by staying in the nursery and paying attention to the tears. The nursery volunteer therefore tries to get the mother to change her behavior.

This way of thinking about problem definitions and solutions is one of several ways that psychologists and pastoral-care practitioners think about frames. A frame is an analysis of a challenge, and the analysis in turn shapes our understanding of the situation and informs our response. Sometimes our frames lock us into cycles of nonproductive or negative behavior, such as that of the child and mother in the nursery; these ineffective frames can be changed when we redefine the situation by targeting the failed solution instead of the presenting symptom, understand people's behavior in a new way, and then try new solutions.[12]

Often this approach to frame analysis is used in the context of one-to-one human interaction. It can also be used to address self-perpetuating, systemic situations in a congregation or other organization, and many pastors and congregational leaders find this approach quite useful as they analyze circumstances in which solutions that seem perfectly logical do not seem to be effective.

Frames as Perspectives

A fourth approach to frame analysis comes from the academic discipline of organization development. In this approach, frames are perspectives—ways of seeing or standpoints from which people examine and deal with life in organizations.

Have you ever been caught in a meeting at church when the participants seem to be at cross-purposes? Someone—let's call her Susan—is concerned that the senior-high kids are not as engaged with the church as she thinks they should be; she worries about their sense of belonging, and she is concerned that older adults pay too little attention to the youth and their programs. Another person in the room, Irene, responds by asking whether they should think about restructuring the children and youth committee. But that isn't what Susan wants. She is concerned that there isn't a place for the kids, that they feel marginalized. For her it's not about a committee—it's about the kids. But Irene doesn't get it. She tackles problems differently and thinks in different categories. For her, if the church can get its structures reoriented or develop the right program, then maybe it can find a workable solution to this serious challenge. It's as if Susan and Irene speak two different languages.

They do. They speak the language of two different frames, two ways of organizing and thinking about their lives as church members. For Susan, church is people and relationships. But Irene finds more of a home in the church's formal structure and systems.

Organization development scholars Lee Bolman and Terrence Deal suggest that their academic discipline uses at least four frames to analyze organizations and their leaders: structural, human behavioral, political, and symbolic.[13] They demonstrate in their work that these frames are particular, focused perspectives that shape how people understand, lead, and work in organizations, and they argue that effective leadership requires the ability to move back and forth between these perspectival frames.

Pastors and other congregational leaders may be familiar with this approach to frame analysis. Some seminary classes introduce this approach in courses on leadership. The authors of *Studying Congregations* use a similar frame analysis to organize their 1998 handbook on congregational studies.[14] Church leadership literature occasionally draws on this approach, too.[15] Many people may be conversant with it.

Four Approaches

Admittedly, these four approaches are not completely distinct. All share in common an understanding of a frame as an interpretive concept that helps people understand and organize their experience in meaningful ways. Yet each approach emphasizes a different way that framing can work.

- Boundary frames work by using brackets that delineate the extent and shape the nature of an experience or event.
- Discursive frames work through metaphors or other speech acts that express, shape, and evoke particular values or worldviews.
- Problem definition and solution frames work through speech acts that diagnose situations and prescribe solutions.
- Perspectival frames are standpoints from which people understand and act in organizations; they offer a particular angle of vision for interpreting structural, behavioral, political, or cultural dynamics.

I find it easiest to tease apart discussions of framing if I can know from which approach a writer or speaker is drawing.

What is my approach in this book? I work mostly with boundary frames for my analysis. In my discussions of preaching, congregational leadership, and frame change, however, I also use the concept of discursive frames.

Worship as a Frame

Frame analysis is useful as we think about the practice of Christian worship. Most worship services are structured as distinct frames, and various styles of worship are characterized by different framing strategies. Moreover, within worship services pastors and leaders employ a variety of frames as they help worshipers understand what faith means, signal to newcomers what sort of church this is, and shape a congregation's understanding of its role in the world. With a fuller understanding of worship frames and how they function, pastors, musicians, and other worship leaders can be more intentional about planning and conducting worship with their congregations.

Questions for Discussion

1. How have you or other church leaders used the concept of "frame" in your work in congregations?
2. In what sorts of situations have you found framing to be a useful tool for ministry?

CHAPTER 2

Frames Define Action

A worship frame shapes the experiential space in which people can, through the action of the Holy Spirit, apprehend God and the meaning of God's presence in their lives. There is no single or best worship frame. Many frames can facilitate good worship. But all effective frames have this in common: they organize worship in ways that are meaningful to people by defining the nature of the action and shaping worshipers' participation in ways that facilitate their involvement.

In the pages that follow I explain how boundary frames combine a variety of worship brackets to shape worship experiences. For the purpose of comparison I primarily discuss the frames utilized in two worship services that I have analyzed carefully, one at Southminster Church and another at St. Luke Church. These services represent different styles and frames, and I use them to demonstrate how frames work. My discussion of the two services is illustrative. All worship services have frames, no matter what their style. They use varieties of elements that tailor worship experiences in particular ways, depending on how they are combined.

Two Services, Two Frames

Dressed in an alb and stole, the pastor sat in a back corner of the small, intimate sanctuary at St. Luke Presbyterian Church. His eyes were tightly closed as he centered himself with prayer. While he prayed, worshipers arrived and took their seats. They talked

quietly to one another, many continuing the more animated conversations that were going on just outside the sanctuary door. The
music director and choir also entered and took their seats at the
back of the sanctuary, next to the organ and organist.

At 10:00 a.m. sharp, the pastor and lay worship leader walked
together down the short center aisle, and the pastor invited the
congregation to share any announcements people wanted to make
public. When the announcements concluded, the two sat in the
chancel while the organist played a short prelude. The worship
frame continued to unfold; it loosely followed a mid-twentieth-
century Presbyterian worship format that places the sermon at the
end of the service. The choir sang an introit. The lay leader stood
and led the congregation in a responsive call to worship. The congregation sang its opening hymn with gusto. The lay leader offered
an invocation, and together the congregation recited the Lord's
Prayer. All stood and praised God by singing the Gloria Patri—
again, with gusto.

Twenty-four miles north, worship used a different frame in the
service at Southminster, which is modeled after "seeker services"
at churches like Willow Creek, a megachurch in close proximity
to Southminster. The frame began to take shape the minute the
worship leaders left the sanctuary at the conclusion of the 9:00
a.m. traditional Presbyterian service. At that time the leaders for
the second service, who had gathered in the narthex, ran down the
side aisles and began to rearrange the chancel for the 11:00 a.m.
service. They were dressed in slacks and sweaters, and a few carried insulated coffee mugs. They brought out music stands and am-
plifiers, plugged in microphones, set up a soundboard in the pews,
took guitars out of their cases, raised the lid on the grand piano,
and mounted an enormous screen on the wall, just to the left of
the huge cross that hangs permanently at the front of the church.
They scrambled to get everything in place, to allow enough time to
rehearse their music before worship. They rehearsed until 10:50,
when they conferred with the pastor, visited with people who came
forward to converse, and without ceremony lit the candles on the
communion table. The scene was busy and informal.

Worship officially began with a brief piano prelude and a
greeting from the pastor, who for this service wore slacks, a sport

coat, and shirt and tie, instead of the black Geneva gown he had worn for the earlier service. The praise team (a guitarist, a pianist, the lead singer, and four other singers) then took over. The five singers each held a microphone, and they led us in singing three songs. Between the first two songs, the pastor greeted us again and invited us to greet each other. Between the second and third songs the praise team leader told worshipers about the meaning the third song held for her. After we sang, the lay leader read a psalm, and the pastor prayed a prayer of confession on the congregation's behalf, followed by an assurance of pardon that he also delivered.

At the conclusion of both services, several processes closed the frames. At St. Luke the worship frame closed with a congregational hymn, a benediction spoken by the pastor, a farewell sung in unison by the congregation, the departure of the worship leaders as they walked back down the center aisle, and an organ postlude. At Southminster the closing was simpler. The congregation sang a final song, the pastor pronounced a benediction and departed by way of the center aisle, worshipers dispersed, and the pastor talked with people in the narthex. At the same time, the team took down and stored the screen and put away the instruments, music stands, and sound equipment. Sunday morning worship had concluded.

Frames Establish Action

The frames described above function in similar ways. They bring people into worship, establish a space for worship and its actions, and send people out. Because corporate worship does not occur continuously but follows a calendar shaped by Sabbath, fast or feast days, and other observances (e.g., funerals, weddings), it requires, whenever it occurs, processes of beginning and ending, entrance and exit. The process at both ends of worship frames can be important.

Goffman states that the opening portion of a frame is of particular significance, because it establishes the action.[1] Setting the stage is as important in worship as in any other kind of frame. "We have found in our experience that the opening three to five minutes of a worship service usually set the tone for much of what follows and determine how engaged many worshipers will be," write Norma Malefyt and Howard Vanderwell in *Designing Worship Together*.[2] Although they do not use the terminology, Malefyt and Vanderwell, an experienced musician-pastor worship team, speak here of the opening portion of worship, the bundle of elements at the start of a service that set the tone and engage worshipers by signaling that worship is starting, and involving worshipers in its movement.

Goffman describes the closing portion of a frame as "doing less work," because it is easier to end a frame than to initiate it. But the closing portion is not without significance. It provides formal closure to an activity and often recaps what has occurred.[3] In worship, closing moments can be powerful. Tom Long, the Bandy professor of preaching at Emory University and Candler School of Theology, and author of *Beyond the Worship Wars*, identifies strong, joyful closings as one of the nine characteristics of worship in vital and faithful congregations.[4]

One way to understand how frames work is to consider how they set worship apart as a distinct activity, and help people make transitions between daily life and the weekly occasion of worship. Arnold van Gennep, an influential anthropologist who studied ritual practices in Africa in the early twentieth century, developed a theory about rituals of passage that I find helpful in understanding worship frames. Rituals of passage are ceremonies in which participants shift from one status to another. In the Christian tradition, baptism is a ritual of passage through which someone assumes a new identity and establishes new relationships by becoming a member of the body of Christ. Marriage is a ritual of passage through which two people leave their status as single adults, marry, and reconfigure their family structures. Funerals are rituals of passage that help mourners to celebrate someone's life and make the transition from a life shared with a friend or family member to a life bereft of that person's physical presence. In Judaism a bar or bas mitzvah is a ritual of passage through which a young person assumes religious adulthood.

In all these rituals the participants become somehow new: they join a church; they get married and sometimes even change their names; they wrestle with the loss of a significant relationship; they grow up. In his book *The Rites of Passage*, Gennep suggests that the transitions that people make in rituals of passage are akin to moving across national or territorial boundaries. Between countries or regions, he notes, there are often boundary markers, signs that one is moving from one territory to another. Travelers experience a common process as they cross boundaries. They leave a familiar territory, make a transition, and enter a new territory into which they may become incorporated. Many return home, changed somewhat by their journey.[5]

A simple example of traveling that would suit Gennep's description of transitional boundaries is the "ritual" that you and I observe whenever we travel by air. To get on an airplane and go somewhere else, we need to have a destination, a ticket, a boarding pass, and valid identification; sometimes we also need to make preparations for our trip—we pack a suitcase or create an itinerary or make reservations for lodging or recreation. If we travel out of the country, we also need to go through customs with our passports and special forms. Each of the things we do to travel and the people and processes we encounter at airport-security checkpoints, reservation desks, customs, or on the plane are what Gennep would call boundary markers. We encounter them when we embark on our travel, and we re-encounter many of them when we come home. They help us cross literal and figurative boundaries.

The ritual of passage is similar to traveling, Gennep argues. It involves processes of leaving, transformation, and re-entry into one's community of origin. Those processes are marked with particular people, artifacts, or behaviors that function as boundary markers, and they help people to make the ritual transitions that are appropriate.[6]

Worship and Ritual Movement

Weekly worship is not a rite of passage for most people, because it usually does not signify or accomplish a change in their status; but it frequently exhibits the ritual movement that Gennep describes.[7] People leave home or work and come to worship, where they encounter the divine or reflect on God's presence in their lives, and then they return to their daily life.

Worship frames help people move back and forth across the boundaries that separate their busy, everyday lives from the dedicated time and space of corporate worship. The opening portion of a worship frame gathers people together from a variety of social, spiritual, and physical locations, brings them into one place, helps them make the shift from daily life to worship, and focuses them on common activities. Worship's closing reverses the movement of the opening; it sends people out to re-enter the world as disciples of Jesus Christ. Again, this is similar to the ritual movement Gennep describes.[8] After a spiritual journey in the context of worship, people make the transition back to the home from which they have come—everyday life, work, family, and all their joys and challenges. There, God willing, worshipers engage their worlds with deeper faith and trust in God.

There are limits, of course, to a territorial metaphor when it comes to worship, because it exaggerates the distinctiveness of worship in contrast to our everyday life of family, work, home, and routine. On the one hand, it is true that the weekly cycle of corporate worship and the annual cycle of liturgical observances are different from our daily cycle of activities; they stand in juxtaposition to our everyday rhythms and form part of the basic ordo of Christian worship.[9] On the other hand, believers discover that such juxtapositions do not isolate worship but rather integrate it into daily life; worship informs and enriches faith, and not just on Sunday.

Despite its limits, however, the territorial metaphor helps to tease apart the dynamics of worship frames, which exhibit the kind of ritual movement and boundary-marking that I discussed above. Worship frames bring people in, establish a space for worship and its actions, and send people out. These boundary frames are composed of a series of what Goffman called "brackets."[10]

What Is a Worship Bracket?

A worship bracket is a single action or configuration that is part of any frame used in a worship service. Although any service can have mini-frames within the central movements of the service, not all use smaller frames in this way, so I focus here on the worship brackets that are most common—those used to open and close worship in the gathering or dismissal phases of worship.[11] A worship bracket is akin to Gennep's idea about boundary markers—something that signifies people's transition between worship and everyday life.[12] Often a phase of worship comprises several brackets. For example, when they describe the gathering phase of worship, Malefyt and Vanderwell identify several elements that can be used in it, such as prelude, processional, opening sentences, songs, introits, passing of the peace, and liturgical dance.[13] Each of these is a bracket. Goffman suggests that most brackets are spatial or temporal,[14] but in worship they can also be verbal, visual, sonic, somatic, or combinations of two or more qualities. In worship services in which I have participated, a number of brackets are employed, and congregations employ them in diverse ways. A partial list of actions or configurations that can function as worship brackets in the gathering or dismissal phases includes:

Spatial brackets

- Room or building in which worship occurs.
- Seating configuration of the congregation and the positioning of worship leaders in relation to the congregation.
- Entrance and exit practices, including the formality (or lack thereof) with which leaders and worshipers enter or leave the worship space.

Temporal brackets

- Dedicated time for worship.
- Liturgical season.
- Tempo of music, speech, and action.
- Duration of gathering or dismissal phases.

Visual brackets

- See spatial brackets above, many of which have visual dimensions.

- Location and visibility of worship leaders.
- Symbols.
- Liturgical-year colors.
- Architecture of building.
- Gender, age, race, or ethnicity (leaders, ushers, greeters, and worshipers).
- Attire (worship leaders, ushers, greeters, and worshipers).
- Chancel furnishings (lecterns, tables, fonts, instruments, projection screens, etc.).

Verbal brackets

- Greetings and announcements.
- Liturgical speech (call to worship, invocation, charge, benediction).
- Patterns of liturgical speech (responsive, single voice, unison).
- Expressiveness of liturgical speech (from exuberance to restraint).
- Words spoken by ushers and greeters before and after worship.

Sonic brackets

- Instrumentation.
- Song genres.
- Instrumental music genres.
- Volume.

Somatic brackets

- Demeanor of worship leaders.
- Physical activity of worshipers (sitting, standing, dancing, running, etc.).
- Pace of activity.

A worship frame is constructed by combining a number of brackets. The frames at St. Luke and Southminster, which I described at the beginning of this chapter, are constructed differently through the combination of the particular brackets they utilize:

St. Luke Opening Brackets

Pastor's prayer
Entrance of worshipers
Entrance of musicians
Processional (pastor robed)
Announcements
Organ prelude
Choral introit

Responsive call to worship

Opening hymn (unison, standing)

(congregation sits)
Invocation (lay leader)
Lord's Prayer (unison)
Gloria Patri (unison, standing)
(congregation sits)

Southminster Opening Brackets

Equipment set-up
Rehearsal
Informal arrival of leaders
Informal lighting of candles
Entrance of worshipers
Piano prelude
Greeting from pastor (coat and tie, slacks)
Praise-and-worship song (unison, standing)
Congregational greetings (everybody)
Praise-and-worship song (unison)
Song interpretation (team leader)
Praise-and-worship song (unison)
(congregation sits)
Psalter reading (lay leader)
Confession and assurance (pastor)

St. Luke Closing Brackets

Closing hymn (unison, standing)
Benediction (pastor)
Sung farewell (unison)
Recessional
Organ postlude

Southminster Closing Brackets

Closing hymn (unison, standing)
Benediction (pastor)
Pastor departs down center aisle
Breakdown of worship set

The diverse use of spatial, temporal, verbal, visual, and sonic brackets results in different worship frames.

The opening portion of a worship frame—its gathering phase—defines the action of worship in several ways. It signals how formal or informal a service is likely to be and contributes to the construction of authority in worship. The frame gives emotional signals and makes it clear to worshipers what degree of expressiveness is appropriate in this service. But before it does anything else, the gathering phase invites participants to worship.

Frames Invoke and Invite

At least two dimensions of invitation are at work in any worship frame—one that is directed toward the divine as it invokes and celebrates God's presence, and another that invites and welcomes women, men, and children. The two are delicately intertwined, and many opening worship brackets, like the following stanza from a hymn by Fred Pratt Green, invite both people and God, and remind worshipers why they have come:

> God is here! As we your people
> Meet to offer praise and prayer,
> May we find in fuller measure
> What it is in Christ we share.
> Here, as in the world around us,
> All our varied skills and arts
> Wait the coming of the Spirit
> Into open minds and hearts.[15]

Brackets in the gathering phase invite people into a consciousness of God's presence and direct their focus to the action of God and its meaning for faithful living. But putting an effective invitation together is not always easy, because people come to worship with differing degrees of readiness, openness, familiarity, and religious competence. Some don't need much of an invitation at all. Others need gentle encouragement. Others respond best to prolonged expressions of welcome. Worship leaders respond to this range of human readiness with different invitation strategies, and construct diverse frames that use varying bundles of worship brackets. Yet, despite variation in worship frames, all frames do common invitational work: they invoke and celebrate God's presence, welcome and include worshipers, and help worshipers ready themselves for the service.

The two worship services that I discussed earlier in this chapter use brackets that frame worship theologically, by invoking and recognizing God's presence with prayer and praise. The opening brackets of call to worship, opening hymn, invocation, Lord's Prayer, and Gloria Patri in St. Luke's service emphasize God's presence and goodness. The opening brackets in Southminster's service do that too, with the pastor's greeting, the music and texts of the songs, the Psalter reading, and the prayer of confession and assurance of pardon. Although they use different brackets and combine them in varying ways, these two services both make it clear that God is here.

God is not the only one whose presence is celebrated during the opening brackets of worship. People are welcomed, too, as leaders greet and invite worshipers to seek God's guidance and to offer praise, thanks, and prayer to God. The opening brackets in both services gather people together and remind them of their shared worship work. At St. Luke this occurs as the congregation joins in the call to worship, opening hymn, and prayers. At Southminster the praise-and-worship songs, coupled with warm greetings from the pastor and others, welcome and invite all to worship.

I experienced welcome in another worship frame at an Emergent Church service, where a different set of opening brackets celebrated God's presence and welcomed people to worship. When I arrived, ushers greeted me and encouraged me to enter the sanctuary. As soon as I got inside the door, I found a "worship station" on either side of the entrance and spotted five or six others in the chancel area; I felt free to visit any of these stations where, with art, writing, or silent devotion before a large cross, I could engage in reflection and prayer. At the same time I heard quiet, calming instrumental music and saw scenes drawn from nature projected on a screen in the front of the sanctuary. Each of these boundary markers reminded me that God was present and accessible to me, and encouraged me to pray or rest in God's presence. In a few minutes, corporate worship began with the leader's welcome and the congregation's participation in opening song, and my individual reflection was redirected toward common action. With other participants I was invited into worship with brackets that engaged ears, eyes, body, and spirit.

I brought something to worship, too—I wasn't a blank slate. As a lifelong churchgoer, I brought my experience, competence as a worshiper, and personal needs, joys, and concerns. I was ready and eager to worship, because it's part of my regular routine. Not everyone engages worship as I do; we each bring our own history and experience to worship. It is the work of opening worship frames to gather individuals in our particularity into the corporate act of worship.

Other worship style frames, such as frames for Taizé worship, exuberant African American worship, or specialized worship services like funerals or weddings, employ different bracketing strategies. In the end, however, effective worship frames are ones that succeed in drawing a congregation together in God's presence and focusing participants' attention on the worship of God.

Frames Establish Formality

Worship frames do more than invoke and invite divine and human participants to worship. Frames also shape the degree of formality a service will have. As worship leaders select and order brackets to frame a worship service, they make decisions that affect how formal worship is. Does the pastor wear a robe or alb, or is she dressed like the worshipers? Is there a formal procession of leaders as worship opens, or do the leaders take their seats with worshipers before the service? How do ushers and worship leaders conduct themselves, and what signals do they give worshipers about appropriate demeanor? What is the seating configuration in the sanctuary, and how are leaders positioned in relation to worshipers? How restricted is access to the equipment (microphones, musical instruments, furniture) or sacramental elements that leaders handle? Which leaders have voice and visibility during the opening brackets of worship?

Every worship leader answers these questions in her own way, and her answers construct the frame that, in turn, influences the level of formality that characterizes worship. Some frames create an almost rigid formality with robed leaders, grand entering and departing processions, solemn demeanors, clergy-only access to leadership roles and materials, and front-facing cathedral seating, which focuses attention on the leaders. Other worship frames are much looser, characterized by informal dress and entrance or exits, relaxed demeanors, broader access to leadership roles and materials, and a circular or semicircular community pattern for seating, which allows worshipers to see each other as well as the leaders.[16] Of course, many worship services fall somewhere between these two extremes.

Many brackets construct social distance between leaders and worshipers; that is, they emphasize the elite position of worship leaders and the relatively less elite position of worshipers. Brackets that place worship leaders in restricted areas like the chancel, put restricted equipment like microphones into their hands, or set leaders apart with distinctive dress each establish social distance. By constructing social distance, such brackets first create mystery and awe, and produce a sense of the sacred.[17] Second, they impute "sacred integrity" to worship leaders.[18] By constructing social distance, brackets like these also contribute to the level of formality that characterizes a worship service. Services in which worship leaders hold restricted, elite positions tend to be more formal because the roles that constrain individual behavior are more tightly drawn.[19] More constraint generally leads to more formality.

In discussions about worship, formality is sometimes confused with authority. It is a mistake, however, to equate the two. Although formality contributes to authority for leaders, it does not automatically result in such authority, nor does informality inevitably lead to dispersed authority. Authority for worship leaders is shaped by several dynamics in addition to the level of formality or informality. Other factors include clerical office and ordination status of leaders, the exercise of that office in worship, the role and visibility of other leaders in worship, the degree of leader-restricted use of equipment or space, displays of piety (often a role for praise teams), and displays of knowledge and expertise (often a role for preachers or teachers). In addition, the use of liturgical elements such as hymns, litanies, creeds, and ancient prayers can subtract authority from leaders; the degree to which such elements are present in worship shapes authority for leaders by drawing it away from them and locating it in the larger tradition.[20]

By shaping the degree of formality that characterizes a worship service and contributing to the authority of worship leaders, a worship frame establishes a tone for worship. That tone is also characterized by emotional expressiveness. A worship frame has an impact on that, too.

Frames Signal Emotion Norms

The praise band is the first thing I notice in a contemporary, seeker-oriented worship service. Loud, active, joyful, and inviting, the group of singers leads the first third of the worship service with energy and excitement. A member of a praise team described her work to me. "You're making a presentation, you know, to [the worshipers]. They can see it, and they're much more a part of it. . . . [We are] giving them the gas to go, in a sense."

Another described it this way: "[We are] physically there to remind you of the joy of what you're doing, to see the emotion. We always laugh because we're always crying. But I think the second any of us feels it, it's just an instantaneous connection to see that, to see someone feeling the Spirit. It just spreads. It spreads among everyone. And so I think that's the benefit of having someone up front. It's to help spread the feeling of the Spirit, to share."

What these team members describe is their responsibility for modeling and, in a sense, producing the appropriate emotional expression for worship. They initiate and lead the opening brackets of worship, and the demands on them are high. They set the tone and tempo, model the joy and openness that they expect from worshipers, and thus establish the appropriate demeanor for worship. They are a significant part of this style's frame.

Leaders of traditional worship feel similar pressures, except that the emotional expression they are expected to model and produce is reserve. I recently went to a committee meeting at the church I attend, which practices a highly formal, traditional version of Presbyterian worship. As the committee members gathered, an old friend of mine kissed my cheek and gave me a hug. "I'm going to give you a kiss," he said, "because I can't do that on Sunday morning in the center aisle!" This man ushers regularly in our church, and he rightly understands that in this congregation it would be inappropriate for an usher—especially one as visible as he is—to hug and kiss a worshiper as she finds her seat. In another congregation, maybe, but not this one.

What's that all about? What's wrong with giving an old friend a kiss? Nothing is wrong, in a general sort of way, but Sunday worship isn't a general sort of thing. In every congregation weekly worship takes a particular form, and that form is defined in part by the emotional contours of the worship experience. In the congregation where I worship those contours tend to be tightly drawn; emotional restraint is the order of the day.

Whatever its style or expression, worship is an emotional experience. It touches our hearts as well as our minds, and at times it connects us with our deepest pains or fears or joys. It can be very powerful. But churches and worship styles express emotion quite differently.[21] Some worship services are highly demonstrative and evocative of visible emotion. Others restrain the expression of emotion. Many are somewhere in between these two extremes.

One of the mistakes observers make is to assume that worship that is more demonstrative has emotion, and worship that is undemonstrative does not. Nothing could be further from the truth. Worship is jam-packed with emotion; differences in worship experiences result from the emotion norms in place, not the emotional depth of the experience.[22]

Emotion norms are expressed and modeled during the opening brackets of worship frames. Such norms are always implicit. No one ever says in public, "Feel this way," or "Display your feelings in this manner," although in private new worship leaders may receive such explicit instructions from more experienced leaders. Instead, emotion norms are signaled in public action through sonic and visual/somatic brackets—particularly instrumental music, song, and the attire and role modeling of worship leaders.

Sonic Brackets

The musicians who were interviewed in the course of my congregational research spoke often about the capacity of music to evoke feelings, especially at the beginning of worship. One talked about his strategy for selecting opening hymns that would energize people. Praise team members, some of whom are quoted above, spoke of demonstrating, igniting, and spreading feeling. An organist in another church reflected on the power of music to set the appropriate tone throughout worship. "The end goal is the experience," he said.

Congregational song plays a significant role in defining emotion norms in worship. Song genres provide markers for worshipers that indicate worship styles and expectations of expressiveness.[23] For example, worshipers get a message about appropriate expressiveness even before worship begins at Trinity UCC in Chicago, as they join the song leader in call-and-response singing, accompanied by drums and keyboard that set a lively, energetic pace. Worshipers get a different message and display emotion differently in congregations where hymn singing is the norm; with its steadier rhythms and four-part harmonies, standard hymnody signals traditional denominational worship for many and sometimes characterizes services that are more reserved in affect. A still different message comes through in congregations like Vineyard churches that sing praise-and-worship music from publishers like Maranatha! Music or Integrity's Hosanna! Music in the opening frame. Here livelier expression is appropriate and modeled by leaders. Song genres alone send messages. Within genres, individual songs or hymns have their own emotional contours.

Visual/Somatic Brackets

As worship opens, visual/somatic brackets also serve to signal emotion norms. These brackets are configurations or actions through which leaders model the appropriate degree of expressiveness for worship in that congregation. When it comes to emotional expressiveness, leaders' role modeling has a strong effect on worshipers.

Goffman observes that in activities in which people are operating with shared emotion norms, whoever initiates interaction is likely to display the demeanor that is normative for that activity. Others, then, tend to take her lead and display a similar demeanor. As people mutually accept and thereby reinforce the demeanor of the occasion, the tone of the initial encounter continues.[24]

In a worship context, the job of initially presenting appropriate demeanor for worship falls to the leaders who set the stage for worship: pastors, lay leaders, ushers, and musicians. It is this group of people who, through their attire and behavior, give the formal and informal cues that signal emotion norms to worshipers.[25] That's why my friend in the center aisle can't give me a kiss. Part of his role as an usher is to cue me and others about the reserve that is appropriate for our congregation's worship service, and in our church a kiss would be a miscue. That is also why praise team members are trying to give people "the gas to go." They seek to produce the feeling and demeanor they believe are appropriate for worship.

An important dimension of emotion role modeling in worship is self-restraint. The worship leaders I interviewed all insist that good worship leadership draws attention to God, not to the leader. In fact, the best worship leadership gets "out of God's way," as one pastor said, and allows the Holy Spirit to direct worship. This approach requires self-control. Worship leaders feel that it is important to put the needs of the congregation before their own needs as they conduct worship. They cannot afford to be distracted by their own levels of exhaustion, personal concerns, the facial expressions of congregational members who seem displeased, a glance from someone who they know is going through a difficult time, the antics of their children, or anything else. Pastors and musicians need to be leaders in and for the congregation for the entirety of worship. Several report that such leadership is costly.[26]

Although worship leaders model and manage emotion throughout the service, the work they do in this regard during opening brackets is of utmost importance, because it sets the tone for worship, lets worshipers know what to expect, and implies how expressive worshipers should be. Effective frames are remarkably successful in their ability to shape worship's emotion norms. Anyone who has ever attended a worship service that exhibits an unfamiliar emotional style knows this to be true. Think how quickly a worshiper who is accustomed to lively, highly expressive worship adjusts when she enters a traditional, formal worship service. A multitude of signals from leaders in the opening brackets let the worshiper know that she should keep her feelings to herself. The reverse is also true. Reserved worshipers often find themselves clapping and moving to new rhythms when they visit lively, expressive worship services. They may not feel quite at home, but the opening brackets of worship make clear what is expected of them. Worshipers pick up these cues and respond appropriately because the framing has worked.

Through a series of brackets that mark boundaries, worship frames shape the experience of participants in profound ways. Frames invite people into worship, create an atmosphere for that experience, and send people out again into the world. In addition, the opening brackets of worship frames also establish formality and signal the emotion norms for worship in that congregation. In doing these things, worship frames establish action. They help worshipers know what is going on and how to participate appropriately.

Questions for Discussion

1. Take a look at a typical order for worship in your congregation. What brackets constitute the gathering and dismissal phases?
2. How does your gathering phase invite God and worshipers to the service?
3. How formal is your worship service, and which brackets shape that formality?
4. What are your congregation's emotion norms for worship? What do leaders do to establish those norms in a typical service?

CHAPTER 3

Frames Focus Attention

As we saw in chapter 2, the opening portions of worship frames establish action. They invoke and invite participants to worship, set the level of formality, and signify the emotion norms for worship. Frames help people enter worship. In this chapter we continue this conversation with reflection on how frames also foster worshipers' involvement by helping them concentrate. The gathering phase of worship focuses people's attention by giving them opportunities to participate actively and directing their thoughts and actions toward the divine. As worship closes, the dismissal phase turns their attention to the world and focuses them on discipleship. In between the two, mini-frames set apart particular segments of worship and aid worshipers with interpretation or transition. To set the stage for this chapter, however, a more general conversation about attention and distraction in worship is needed.

The Importance of Concentration

In *With All Thy Mind*, Robert Glick, associate professor of church music and worship at Erskine College and Theological Seminary, reflects on two experiences he had as he worshiped at Cambridge University chapels. At King's College, in a crowded worship service attended by many tourists, he found himself almost unable to worship.

As evensong progressed, I noticed a restlessness in the crowded chapel. People were fidgeting with their shopping bags and cameras, whispering to their neighbors, and straining to look all around. Many were not actively involved in saying the prayers or the creed. It felt to me as though many were there merely to see the show and not to participate in worship. At least in part because of the weakness of my own faith, I found it difficult to concentrate on the worship of God in such an environment.[1]

Glick had a dissimilar experience at St. John's College, when his attention was caught by a man sitting nearby, one of the few people in attendance:

I could not help but notice the intensity of his participation through all aspects of the service. His effect on me was involved. After I had just come from the large semi-involved crowds at King's College, this young man silently communicated to me a humble, devout piety which made it much easier for me to focus on worship, and I felt less alone. By the power of his apparent sincerity of prayer and genuine praise, he ushered me into the presence of the Almighty.[2]

Glick raises many significant issues with these stories. I want to focus on one: how important it is for worshipers to be able to concentrate on worship, and how annoying it can be when aspects of worship are distracting. This may seem a rather obvious statement, but there is more to it than is immediately apparent.

Glick is not the only student of worship to observe how important it is to focus attention and avoid distraction in worship. Tom Long, for example, speaks of the strength that a good narrative order can bring to worship and the responsibility of leaders to conduct worship in ways that allow the different pieces to connect. He also describes how a familiar repertoire of resources can facilitate a flow of worship that is vital and faithful.[3] Malefyt and Vanderwell urge worship planners to ensure thematic coherence in worship. In addition, when they suggest ways that worship can be evaluated, they make it clear that good worship should avoid things like chaotic orders of service, unclear bulletins, distracting announcements and music, and disjointed flow and transitions—all of which can divert worshipers' attention.[4]

No one speaks more strongly about the need for concentration and the annoyance of distractions than worshipers themselves. Goffman observes, as have others, that paying attention is what is expected from people in church. It is situationally appropriate for people to be engaged and to maintain an appropriate demeanor as they worship.[5] Although that is undoubtedly true, data from my interviews indicate that people pay attention not only because that is what is expected of them, but also because they want to. Paying attention is the effort that worshipers say they need to make in order to worship meaningfully.

The psychologist Mihaly Csikszentmihalyi has found that the capacity of people to pay attention correlates with their level of satisfaction in an experience.[6] In fact, attention and satisfaction are synergistic. Being able to concentrate allows people to be more fully involved in an experience, and that involvement is enhanced as the experience supports people's ability to pay attention.[7] Csikszentmihalyi takes this argument further and states that people experience deep satisfaction in experiences in which they are fully engaged, and are able to use and expand their skills, meet challenges, and build their self-confidence. He characterizes the experience of being fully immersed in a gratifying activity as "flow."[8]

Basketball coach Phil Jackson and journalist Malcolm Gladwell make similar points about the connection between attention and satisfaction. In his memoir *Sacred Hoops*, Jackson describes the almost transcendent experience that basketball players have when they use their mental, physical, and spiritual resources to play in harmony with one another. When that attentiveness occurs, the players, team, and game rise above themselves in ways that produce deep satisfaction for them.[9] In reflections of another sort, Gladwell discusses the impact of intense involvement on what he calls "stickiness"—factors that make some experiences more memorable than others. He notes that in studies about children and television, researchers have concluded that the more deeply involved children were in a television show, the more significant and unforgettable that show seemed to be.[10] Attention and satisfaction are connected.

Worship ADD

Worship, admittedly, is neither basketball nor children's TV, but nonetheless concentration makes a difference. In *every* interview I conducted, worshipers identified paying attention as their primary responsibility in worship. I was astonished. Not only was I surprised at the consistency of people's responses—I had expected more variation—but I was surprised that paying attention was so important to them. The more I looked at my fuller conversations with these people, the more evidence I saw that reinforced their assertions.[11]

People may want to concentrate during worship, but not everyone finds it easy to do that. In fact, many people told me that they find it challenging to pay attention in worship. Some people have short attention spans and are easily detoured. "I can get distracted by just staring at the window," said one man. It is not only people like him who admit, "I truly am ADD" (attention-deficit disordered), who find it difficult to pay attention in worship. Many do.

The biggest distraction that people face is what they carry in—everyday challenges, problems, and pressures. Two-thirds of those I interviewed talked about their struggle to put aside the concerns that fill their mind as they worship. They also talked about how worship itself can aid or disrupt concentration.

People say that they concentrate best in worship when they know and understand why something is there and what it means and can engage it meaningfully. When worship includes something they don't understand or that makes them uncertain, some people admit that they "zone out," as one person said. Sermons that fail to get to the point or that are too theologically technical impede concentration; they make people feel inadequate, even dumb, and those feelings disrupt worship. Equally troubling are songs or hymns that the congregation doesn't know and that are difficult to sing or have complex texts. Being asked to sing a new song is distressing to many, because it causes a disconnection for them and makes people feel self-conscious. One person told me about his response to singing an unknown hymn: "I hated it. It was unfamiliar. I couldn't find the melody. It seemed like I was out of sync as I sang, like the organ was playing something entirely different from what we sang." A woman said she feels "very left out" when she cannot follow a tune in a praise song and does not have the music. Another said she feels "like a complete idiot" when she cannot follow the melody in a praise song.

Knowing what comes next in worship makes a difference, too, because then people can worship without worrying about making a mistake. For some worshipers any break in the continuity is distracting. Consequently they appreciate services that are coherent, in which there are connections between all the parts. Some appreciate worship most when a central theme holds the service together. Others appreciate leaders who conduct worship smoothly. A leader who is nervous and self-conscious, ill-prepared, or a poor speaker can distract people from worship and make them think instead about the quality of leadership or the flow of worship. One woman stated:

> If the people who are up front know what they're doing and lead people along, there's no problem. It's when people start feeling uncomfortable and afraid of what they're doing because they don't know what comes next. I think the discomfort level gets high and the act of worship is lost. It suddenly becomes, "Can I do this right?" and that's not what it's all about.

Concentration Strategies

What worship is all about, worshipers attest, is having an opportunity to open their hearts to God and hear the messages that are being spoken. Consequently, worshipers work hard to concentrate. They try to close out the outside world, so they can really listen. They do their best to leave their worries behind, so they can focus on "the eternal truths, the eternal verities," as one woman said. People want to worship meaningfully. That's why they are there. "You should get as much out of it as you can—insights, encouragements, new challenges. If you just go and sit and think about other things, that's bad," another woman concluded.

Some people described the strategies they've developed to help them concentrate. One worshiper always sits in the first row, so

she has nothing around her to distract her. Another disciplines herself to leave her difficulties at the door when she worships, so that
her mind can be free to concentrate on God. She also takes notes.
Reminiscent of the psalmist's testimony, "O God, you are my God,
I seek you, my soul thirsts for you. . . . So I have looked upon you
in the sanctuary, beholding your power and glory" (Ps. 63:1-2),
worshipers at two of the churches I studied concentrate by gaz-
ing on the large crosses at the front of their sanctuaries. Several
people report that it is important for them to prepare for worship
with devotional time on Sunday morning. Being able to slow down
and focus on worship before getting there aids their concentration.
One man copes with distraction by saying a prayer. "When you
become aware that you are drifting, pray, 'Lord, take me back,'
and you can come back, but you have to be cognizant of the fact
that you are drifting," he said.[12]

People said they worship to experience, renew, and strengthen
their relationship with God. Paying attention is one part they play,
and they take it seriously. They clear their minds. They focus. They
listen. They put considerable effort into being emotionally and in-
tellectually present, reaching out to God and opening themselves
to receive something. Their responsibility is, in the words of one
worshiper, "to try and block out the rest of the world, to be able
to open my heart to the words and songs of our Lord." When
worshipers are able to do that, they find worship more satisfying,
more memorable, and more meaningful.

Frames Foster Engagement

While worshipers recognize the importance of attention in worship and instinctively devise their own strategies to enhance their
concentration, the actions of worship itself help them pay attention. As people enter a sanctuary and respond to the invitation to
worship, they often participate in song, response, and other vocal-
izations that catch them up in prayer and praise. To put it a little
more crudely, worshipers and leaders make sound together, often
during the first few brackets of worship.

Sound—the spoken and sung word, instrumental music, and silence—is an essential part of worship, and it is a characteristic of frame brackets that helps worshipers pay attention. Sound itself is simply the physical reality produced by the effect of sonic vibrations on the human ear and brain. By its very nature, sound is active, and when two or more are gathered, it is social, too; it is an immediate, dynamic, physical experience in which speakers or musicians and listeners are drawn together. Sound is an invitation to engagement, liturgical musicologist Edward Foley, Capuchin, contends. When people produce and hear sound, they are pulled into the experience—the physical experience of making or receiving sound, the intellectual experience of the meaning that they intend or interpret, and the experience of community (I discuss the relational dimensions of worship in more detail in chapter 4).[13]

In worship people experience sound in a variety of ways. Sometimes worshipers are hearers only, as instrumentalists play sacred music, leaders speak, or the assembly listens in silence for God. At other times worshipers speak or sing in unison or in various responsive forms.[14] How we participate in worship's sound makes a difference, Foley states. When soloists sing or play instruments, or worship leaders speak monologically, the sound event communicates that the speaker is more important than the worshipers, who are positioned as less significant subjects in worship. When leaders and worshipers share in responsive liturgical forms, the sound event also highlights the leaders' visibility, but suggests at the same time that although leaders and worshipers have different roles, they have parity as actors in worship. Engaging the congregation in unison silence, speech, or singing, however, symbolizes that the gathered worshipers are integral to the event and important enough to be considered primary actors in worship.[15] Foley's point is simple: the more actively people participate in worship, the more they are deemed important and the more it becomes their work.

Sound helps people pay attention in worship, because it gives them something to do—listen, speak, sing, respond, keep silent. Sound is sensual; it commands worshipers' hearing and thus their attention, and if they produce sound, it also is a tactile experience that gives voice to their faith. Sound engages worshipers' bodies as well as their minds and hearts, and it makes them aware of each other. The more intensely worshipers can participate in sound making, the more involved they are likely to be in worship, because they are doing it themselves, not just watching or hearing it.

Opening brackets of worship regularly encourage people to voice their faith by providing opportunities for them to join in responsive or unison song and speech. This is part of the logic that stands behind the extended praise-and-worship music set that characterizes worship in the Vineyard Church, where congregational singing is designed to woo people into worship. As people sing through the set, they get involved in the service; move through the five stages of invitation, engagement, exultation, adoration, and intimacy; leave behind whatever distracts them; and ready themselves to enter the "holy of holies" at the heart of worship. The music set focuses participants' attention.[16]

Other worship services display bracketing strategies that also seek to focus people's attention through active, vocal participation. Earlier we looked at the opening worship frame at Southminster, which resembles the Vineyard format, though with significant variations. One Sunday in Lent the congregation was ushered into worship with this opening (portions said or sung in unison are indicated by italics; the congregation was also standing for the unison elements of worship):

- Rehearsals and entrances
- Prelude (piano)
- Welcome
- *Songs of praise*
- *Greeting*
- *Song of praise*
- Psalter reading
- Prayer of confession, silence, and assurance of pardon
- *Song of thanks*

Note the balance between leader-led elements of worship and unison participation in this opening frame—it's about fifty-fifty. Significant portions of this opening frame allow the entire congregation to participate, and the sequential ordering of most of the unison elements intensifies the sense of participation and action for people. They are singing or greeting each other, and making worship happen by their participation; they know they are involved and valued as participants; and they are paying attention.

I do not want to suggest that people fail to pay attention when they listen quietly in worship. My research indicates the opposite: listening can be an active experience for worshipers, and many enjoy the quieter moments of worship, which give them opportunities for contemplation. Worshipers pay plenty of attention when they are quiet, and they appreciate the chance to do so. My point is simply that quiet listening engages fewer senses than does singing or speaking (both of which also involve listening in addition to other physical efforts involved in producing sound); making sound thus involves people more fully than does simply listening.

Opportunities for participation are also provided in opening brackets at St. Luke. (Again, unison portions are indicated by italics. Individual worshipers made some of the announcements. The people stood for the hymn and Gloria Patri.)

- Entrances (including a brief processional)
- Announcements
- Prelude (organ)
- Introit (choir)
- Call to worship
  L: I stand up straightest when I bend to help.
  P: I speak loudest when I listen to another.
  L: The more I give away the more I have.
  P: I am more human when I find the Divine.
  L: Praise God.
  P: Praise God in the sanctuary
- *Hymn*
- Prayer of invocation
- *Lord's Prayer*
- *Gloria Patri*

Like the opening brackets at Southminster, those used in St. Luke's service evenly balance leader-led and responsive or unison

participation. Here, however, instead of concentrating unison participation primarily in one portion of the opening frame, as occurred at Southminster, participation builds somewhat differently,
from a few individuals participating in the announcements, to
the responsive call to worship, to the unison hymn, and finally to
back-to-back opportunities for unison participation in the Lord's
Prayer and Gloria Patri. The participation of the gathered assembly intensifies as this opening frame unfolds.

Worship frames focus attention by giving people worship
work to do. Opening brackets welcome worshipers' participation
in song, response, and prayer, and they engage multiple senses as
individuals join their hearts and voices in praise of God.

Frames Do Theological Work

Perhaps the most important function of a worship frame is the
theological orientation it provides, which promotes concentration
by focusing worshipers on their relationship with God. Frames
include multiple elements that make theological statements about
who human beings are, who God is, and the connection between
humans and the divine. Theological framing occurs at the beginning and end of worship, and it is shaped by bracketing strategies
that order elements in particular ways and discursive strategies
that make theological claims. As I discuss theological framing,
readers will note that the tidy, neat distinctions that I drew between boundary and discursive frames in chapter 1 are blurred in
actual practice because many brackets have words. The following
conversation about framing therefore includes both the boundary
and discursive work that frames do.

Opening worship frames do discursive work, because they remind worshipers of God and God's covenant with human beings.
In the worship frame at Southminster, an example of which is reproduced earlier in this chapter, people sang four songs: "As We
Gather," "Awesome Power," "Come and Fill Me Up," and—after
the reading of Psalm 33:18-22, the prayer of confession, and the
assurance of pardon—"Oh, How He Loves You and Me." The
first three songs called people to worship, invoked God's presence,

and invited people to allow God to bless and work within them. These songs addressed God in the second person or as "Holy Spirit" or "Lord," and characterized God as having power, grace, mercy, truth, love, and righteousness. The last two songs framed the psalm, prayer of confession, and assurance of pardon; "Come and Fill Me Up" sang of worshipers' need for God and asked God to wash away their sins. "Oh, How He Loves You and Me" did not name God or Christ specifically, but thanked God for giving God's life for worshipers.

As worshipers sang these songs, they positioned themselves theologically as people who are in a loving relationship with God and as sinners who need God's forgiveness. God is good and powerful, a trusted divine presence who can be known intimately. These affirmations were deepened as participants listened to the psalm, prayer of confession, and assurance of pardon. By the time the opening worship frame concluded, worshipers had declared their faith and claimed their dependence on a loving, reliable God. They had also voiced their praise, gratitude, and love for God.

The example of the opening frame at St. Luke, reproduced above, made similar theological claims, although the language employed in this example was less intimate than that used at Southminster.[17] In this service, too, worshipers reminded themselves of who they were in relationship with God. After declaring that they were more human when they discovered God, worshipers joined in singing "Praise, My Soul, the King of Heaven," a hymn that includes multiple images of God's care for human beings, who are characterized as saved, forgiven, rescued, healed, and gently nurtured by God. In this hymn God, who is referred to in the third person, is not only a "King" but also "fatherlike," kind, protective, gracious, and magnificent in glory. All are called to give praise. Human dependence, God's mercy, nurture, forgiving grace, and glory were declared again as worshipers joined in the Lord's Prayer and Gloria Patri.

With the language, music, and types of interaction they employ, frames do theological work. The discursive content of many opening brackets allows worshipers to stand honestly before God, state their need for God's presence in their lives, and offer praise and prayers that celebrate God's power, goodness, and grace. In a culture that celebrates self-sufficiency and human accomplishment, such convictions are important to voice. As Christians we understand ourselves as creatures, dependent on God for every breath we take. We are sinners redeemed through the grace of God in Jesus Christ. The opening brackets of worship remind us of this truth and give us space to name it.

Frames can do this theological work in various ways. Two worship services that I experienced at McCormick Theological Seminary illustrate how different frames do similar work. McCormick is related to the Presbyterian Church (U.S.A.), but about half of its students come from other denominational traditions. Several years ago I worked with a team of students to prepare a worship service, and I asked a Baptist student to prepare the prayer of confession, which is normally part of the opening frame in Presbyterian services. She balked, explaining that it was not part of her tradition, and saying she didn't really understand what I was talking about. We worked together, and despite her struggles she did a fine job, but all the while she kept insisting that her tradition did not include anything like this.

A few weeks later she and other Baptist students, who represented several different streams of their tradition (Missionary Baptist, National Baptist, and American Baptist), fashioned a service that they said was more typical of their denominations. We sang some new songs, and the service did not include a prayer of confession in the opening frame. The service did, however, open with a leader offering a prayer that began, "God, we thank you that you are God and we are not." The prayer continued with an acknowledgment of what God does every day for human beings: God wakes us up, gives us a new day, provides for our needs, loves us despite our sin and failings, and is present in our lives in a multitude of ways.

These services looked and felt very different from one another. The two frames employed different liturgical resources, patterns of leadership and congregational participation, and selection and ordering of elements. The frames also included somewhat different theological language, but ultimately they did similar work. Both frames invoked God's presence, invited worshipers to participate, established a level of formality, signaled emotion norms, involved participants in various songs and prayers, and made theological claims about God, human beings, and our relationship with each other.

"God, we thank you that you are God and we are not." In my mind, this prayer sums up the theological work that opening frames do in worship. Sometimes, as in Presbyterian orders for worship, human sinfulness and our need for God's forgiving grace are stressed. At other times, as in the service that our students planned and led, the emphasis falls more on God's abiding grace and goodness in human life. But in the end a similar point is made in every worship frame: God is God, and we are not, and every day we have ample reason to thank and praise God.

The fullness of the relationship between humans and the divine can never be stated in a single worship service or frame. Throughout the church year various aspects of our relationship with God are emphasized in worship and articulated in opening frames. *The Book of Common Prayer* of the Episcopal Church suggests an opening frame for morning worship that includes sentences of Scripture, confession of sin, assurance of pardon, invitatory, and Psalter. The sentences of Scripture, invitatory, and Psalter change through the liturgical year, and the theological emphases in these brackets differ, too. In Advent, for example, the themes of hope and expectation are voiced with an opening sentence such as "Prepare ye the way of the Lord; make straight in the desert a highway for our God"; and an invitatory like "Our King and Savior draweth nigh: O come, let us adore him." Contrast this with the more celebratory and joyful tone of one of Easter's opening sentences, "Thanks be to God, which giveth us the victory through our Lord Jesus Christ," and invitatory, "Alleluia. The Lord is risen indeed: O come, let us adore him. Alleluia."[18] Although they may have different emphases and moods, and may be embodied differently as priests opt to speak or sing the liturgy, these frames do similar theological work. They highlight themes in the Christian story, recall worshipers' relationship with God, and invite people to adoration and faith.

Opening frames focus people's concentration not only by involving them in doing worship work, but also by articulating theological convictions that direct their attention to God. With reminders of how human beings are dependent on God, brackets in the gathering phase of worship help people remember God's gifts, trust God's promises, and open themselves to God's continuing guidance and grace.

Frames Encourage Discipleship

Closing brackets help worshipers pay attention, too, but they focus concentration on everyday living instead of corporate worship. The dismissal phase of worship thus reverses the action of the gathering phase. As worship opens, frames pull people in and focus them on the shared worship work that will occur during the service. Closing brackets, on the other hand, conclude corporate action, focus attention outward, remind worshipers of God's call and companionship, and send people out to serve God in the world.

Although he does not use the term "frame," Long, in analyzing services that end with a joyful and celebrative spirit, affirms that the goal of the concluding frame of worship is to send worshipers into the world as renewed followers of Christ.[19] To accomplish this sending, concluding frames do theological work. They give worshipers an opportunity to commit themselves to God, charge them to share their faith, and offer a benediction that reminds people of God's blessings and promises of peace.

The closing frame at the church where I normally worship begins with the offering, a tactile act that provides people an opportunity to give something to God. The gift is a financial one, but my pastors often characterize money as a symbol of other riches that we can bring to God—riches of time and talent. I experience this portion of worship as an opportunity to commit money and myself to God.

Following the offering, as ushers bring forward the gifts, the congregation stands and sings a response by Carl P. Daw that the church commissioned several years ago:

For the life that you have given,
For the love in Christ made known,

With these fruits of time and labor,
With these gifts that are your own:
Here we offer, Lord, our praises,
Heart and mind and strength we bring.
Give us grace to love and serve you,
Living what we pray and sing.[20]

A unison prayer of thanksgiving and dedication follows, and we conclude the service with a hymn, benediction, choral response, and organ postlude. These brackets send worshipers into the world with a gentle, theological reminder that all of their gifts belong to God and are given for faithful living. The hymn and benediction remind worshipers of God's presence in worship and throughout their lives. All are encouraged to depart in peace, as disciples upheld by God's care and presence.

Church musician and liturgical scholar Michael Hawn describes a similar movement of worship in a different church. Grace Church's motto is "Out of many, God makes us one." The concluding brackets of the congregation's worship reflect the congregation's commitment to building unity from human diversity, and hint that this vocation follows church members into the world. The weekly celebration of the Lord's Supper draws the congregation together around a common table and faith, and Hawn reports that people from many cultures break bread together. At the conclusion of worship another closing bracket, which was written by Carol St. George, a member of the congregation, expresses Grace's commitment to unity in Christ. Each week worshipers at Grace close worship by singing:

Praise to thee, O Joyous spirit, God of beauty, God of love,
Send us forth in love and service with the grace that makes us
    one.
Sanctify our daily living; grant us strength of heart and soul.
In God's likeness we, united, share the peace that makes us
    whole.

Immediately following worship the congregation enjoys a time of fellowship, which brings together its membership into another common activity and also symbolizes its dedication to diverse Christian community. That commitment to creating unity through faith, says Hawn, is Grace. Its dismissal phase closes worship with several brackets—communion, song, and fellowship—that remind people what the congregation stands for and how the church hopes its members will engage the world.[21]

At the close of a worship frame, attention shifts. Through a series of actions, people prepare to enter their everyday lives again. Closing brackets encourage them to be disciples and remember that God is always with them.

Mini-Frames and Attention

Brackets used as frames in the midst of worship can aid concentration, too. When worshipers talked with me about what they found distracting or troubling in worship, among the things they mentioned were not being able to understand something and not knowing what was coming next in the service. They told me that these sorts of experiences were frustrating because they interfered with worship. Frames can be used to avoid experiences that frustrate people by instead focusing worshipers' concentration with strategies that define the boundaries of particular segments of worship (such as a sacrament or the sermon) or that help worshipers make transitions.

Smaller worship frames—what I'm calling mini-frames—can be used to make portions of worship stand out as distinct. For example, the children's sermon in many congregations is defined by a mini-frame. As I have seen it practiced, the children's message is framed with an invitation for the children to leave their seats and come forward to the chancel; when the message is concluded, sometimes with a prayer, the children are dismissed and return to their seats or go to Sunday school. The physical movement of the children, coupled with the discursive invitation, prayer, and concluding remarks of the leader, form a mini-frame that gives boundaries to the children's message. This mini-frame helps children and adults know what's happening. Participants understand that this is a special time for the children, during which things may be a little different from the remainder of the service. Children understand that this is their special time with the leader, and many understand that different rules apply; youngsters may, for instance, be able to talk out loud during this portion of worship instead of whisper or keep silent, as they are encouraged to do in the rest of the service. The mini-frame around the children's sermon helps to keep these particular boundaries of access to leadership and behavior norms in place for kids and adults.

In at least two congregations in which I've worshiped, sermons are bracketed with mini-frames. At Southminster the children leave worship before the sermon and move to the chapel, where they hear a children's message and identify their joys and concerns for prayer. When the sermon concludes, the children return to worship, and their joys and concerns are sometimes shared with the congregation before adults are asked to share in similar ways before prayer. The movement of the children in and out of the service gives boundaries to the sermon.

A second example comes from the congregation in which I worship regularly, where worship is held in a large English Gothic sanctuary. The chancel is raised several steps above the sanctuary floor, and the pulpit is raised several more steps above the chancel. Movement, lighting, and music frame the reading of the second Scripture lesson and the sermon. As the congregation sings the Gloria Patri, the preacher ascends to the pulpit, while light dims in the sanctuary and the spotlights that shine on the preacher are lit. He or she then prays, reads from the Bible, and preaches. When the sermon concludes, the spotlights are dimmed, the sanctuary lights come up, the preacher descends, and the congregation sings a hymn. Obviously, I worship in a church that takes preaching seriously and sets the sermon apart in a rather dramatic way. The mini-frame of song, lighting, and movement focuses worshipers' attention on the preacher and message. It sets apart the sermon from the rest of the worship service.

Mini-frames are regularly used by worship leaders to highlight certain segments of worship in ways that help participants understand what's happening. These frames come with subliminal messages, too, of course. The framing of children's sermons turns adult worshipers into eavesdroppers, because it officially excludes them from participation; it also hints that children are not full participants in the rest of the service. The framing of the sermon at Southminster gives a clear message that sermons are for adults only, while the sermon framing in my congregation literally elevates the authority of the preacher and the word. None of these subliminal messages are inherently negative, but neither are they necessarily deliberate on the part of worship leaders. These messages come as part of the framing package. Nonetheless, these mini-frames do their work: they set apart particular segments of worship as distinct.

Frames can also be used to interpret segments of worship or to help worshipers make transitions from one part of worship to another. Worship leaders routinely introduce some elements of worship. When introductions are habitual and used frequently, they can be brief: "Let us now stand and sing 'Spirit of the Living God.'" Less regular introductions may need to be longer; for example, if a preacher bases a sermon on an obscure biblical text, she may need to provide a more extensive interpretation prior to reading the text, so worshipers can better understand it. A few years ago I preached a sermon about Samson, from a text in Judges. Because I believed that many in the congregation would be unfamiliar with the story, I provided background about Samson before reading the text. When I preach from a gospel text, however, I rarely introduce it, because I think that it will be familiar to most worshipers. Introduction practices, of course, differ from leader to leader and church to church.

Thoughtful introductions and transitional remarks can help to focus worshipers' attention by setting the stage for what comes next or interpreting the movement of worship.[22] Transitions can be especially important for newcomers. I needed transitions like these when I worshiped recently at an Episcopal church, where there were many visitors in the congregation. Those who were unfamiliar with *The Book of Common Prayer* were helped by priests who offered short transitions like "The service continues with Canticle 7 on page 52." Without priestly guidance like this, they would have been completely lost and unable to worship as meaningfully as they did. Introductions or transitions like the one just described are mini-frames that give boundaries to segments of worship, let worshipers know what is coming next, interpret worship segments for people, and establish temporary behavioral norms.

Frames and Worship Leadership

Frames focus attention by orienting worshipers to whatever is coming next. In the opening brackets, attention is focused toward God. With mini-frames, attention is focused on the next segment of worship. In the closing brackets, attention is focused more toward the world. Each frame portion attempts to prepare worshipers to concentrate on the joys, challenges, and tasks at hand. When constructed thoughtfully, worship frames function as they are intended: to pull people together in a common mind and voice at the start of worship, to help them attend throughout worship, and to send them out as faithful disciples at the conclusion.

Worship frames are not static. They are dynamic portions of worship that leaders construct by selecting various brackets, combining them in particular ways, and leading them appropriately. Even in worship traditions that prescribe frames rather tightly, as in *The Book of Common Prayer*, there is latitude for leaders to select various elements, sing or speak the liturgy, and adapt visual, sonic, and somatic brackets such as sanctuary decorations, songs or instrumentation, or entrance practices to suit the congregation's style. In less formal worship traditions there is even more latitude for choice and experimentation.

How leaders decide to construct worship frames has significant consequences for congregations. Frames help people worship more fully by inviting, cueing, and involving them in doing worship work. Frames also do theology, as sociologist Stephen Ellingson demonstrates in his study of nine Lutheran congregations, some of which modified their worship frames. How frames are constructed, Ellingson contends, not only readies people for worship by focusing their concentration; it also shapes the theological identity of a congregation.[23] How frames shape a church's community and affect its theology are topics I address in chapters 4, 5, and 6.

Questions for Discussion

1. How does the gathering phase in your Sunday morning service involve people in responsive or unison participation?
2. What theological claims do worshipers and leaders make during the gathering phase in your church?
3. What does discipleship mean in your congregation, and how is it expressed in the closing frame?

CHAPTER 4

Frames Shape Community

In chapters 2 and 3 I discussed how worship frames help individuals to worship by establishing action, inviting people to participate, getting them involved, and focusing worshipers' attention on God. In this chapter I continue my analysis of worship frames, but shift attention from the individual to the corporate and examine the effect that worship frames can have on congregations. I look again at the work of both boundary and discursive frames in welcoming, letting people know that they belong, and providing theological orientation to a worshiping assembly.

As you and I consider these things, it is important to remember that worship frames are human constructs. That is, people design and make frames. Worship leaders determine how frames are put together, what words are put into worshipers' mouths, and what messages are sent as people participate in worship frames. Once constructed, however, frames can have powerful effects. The impact that worship frames can have on congregations is the subject of this chapter.

Belonging

Among the most important questions that any congregation needs to answer are these: Who belongs? Whom does God call into this particular expression of the body of Christ? These are, at root, theological questions, because how leaders answer them reflects and shapes a congregation's witness to its faith.

I participated once in a conversation with a group of clergy, in which two participants disagreed about how to answer these questions. The conflict began when a pastor announced that her church had no boundaries. "Everyone is welcome," she said. Another member of the group, who served a congregation that had a significant ministry among the gay and lesbian community, became impatient and told her that was nonsense. He insisted that all churches have boundaries and that there is no such thing as a church that welcomes everyone. He knew full well that people who were uncomfortable around gay and lesbian people would decide not to attend his church, and he had made peace with that. He assumed, probably correctly, that the same was true for her church—some people would choose not to be affiliated, for one reason or another. Their choice to attend elsewhere would shape her church's boundaries and limit its capacity to include people.

Looking back on this conversation, I think both pastors were correct. When he argued that a single congregation cannot be all things for all people, the second pastor spoke from his awareness of the effects that human limits and brokenness have on a worshiping community. Every church has implicit boundaries around belonging, many of which are imposed not only by reasonable preferences or restraints (a person living in Los Angeles is unlikely to attend a church in New York every weekend) but also by human sinfulness. Although congregations can and do change those boundaries, this pastor's point is well taken. Every congregation has boundaries that imply who does or does not belong there, and church community is built within them.

The first pastor viewed her congregation differently. Instead of looking at it through the realistic lens of social pluralism and human brokenness, she looked at it through the visionary lens of God's promises. Echoing in her remarks were Isaiah's dream of the holy mountain, Jesus's table fellowship with sinners and outcasts, Paul's convictions about the unity of the Body of Christ, and other biblical texts that proclaim the gracious expanse of God's mercy. She understood rightly that her congregation, like all of ours, was called to stretch toward a biblical vision of unity and to strive for a deeper faithfulness.

Both these pastors spoke the truth. Every congregation lives in the tension that their argument represented: we are limited, sinful people, yet at the same time we are members of God's human family who are called to build communities that transcend our brokenness and exhibit the commonwealth of God to the world.

At its best, worship embodies this paradox. In his book *Holy Things*, Gordon Lathrop, a liturgical theologian, ponders the many ways that worship holds human sinfulness in tension with God's promises. One of the places that occurs, he says, is in the opening frame, when statements of welcome, acts of reconciliation, and participation in shared symbols and actions welcome strangers and remind worshipers of the ways that God has welcomed them.[1]

When worship frames successfully hold people's brokenness and God's promises in tension, they build belonging. By assuring people that God welcomes sinners and rejoices every time the lost are found, frames include both experienced worshipers and strangers in the gathering, and remind them that it is God's grace that has brought them together. The belonging that worship frames help to establish is more than theological, however; it is also practical. As individual congregations share worship practices and symbols, they join the many individuals present in the congregation into a community of faith.

From Many, One

One of the biggest challenges that worship leaders face is determining how to pull together the diversity that exists in the congregation into a single worshiping body. To gather the many into the one is no small feat. Diversity confronts congregations in several guises: religious, demographic and cultural, and personal.

In the twenty-first century religious identity comes in all sorts of shapes, packages, and expressions, and people who were raised in a particular religious tradition do not feel obligated to remain in it. As they move from town to town, or grow dissatisfied with a particular church, many people switch churches and traditions with apparent ease.[2] The combination of variety and mobility results in worshiping congregations whose members have dissimilar religious experience, interests, skills, and aesthetics. Even the most homogeneous congregations are likely to include people with diverse religious backgrounds. In a recent membership analysis of four Presbyterian congregations, whose members are over 90 percent middle-class Caucasian, I found that beginning in the late 1980s and early 1990s, all four began receiving more members who were not familiar with Presbyterianism than members who were. Prior to the late '80s, the reverse had been true—the majority of new members had transferred their membership from other Presbyterian or historic Protestant mainline congregations.[3] Even congregations whose members look similar may struggle with considerable religious dissimilarity beneath the surface.

Congregations are demographically and culturally diverse, too. Not only do the differences between men and women, or adults and children, characterize congregations, but also joined to the mix are different generational styles and cognitive orientations.[4] Some congregations have the added good fortune of being multiracial or multi-ethnic.[5] Every dimension of demographic and cultural diversity contributes to the challenges that church leaders face as they try to form a single worshiping body.

In addition, each congregation includes people with diverse personal needs. One pastor described a typical range of concerns that he considers as he prepares worship each week:

> I'm thinking of a couple of people. I'm thinking of Ann, who was divorced years ago and raised her children all by herself with no support—emotional, physical, financial—at all from her ex-husband. There's a young lady who has never married and is now adopting a child from China. There is John, who is really lonely. I also think of Ruth, who was back in church yesterday after probably a yearlong absence or so, because she really wanted a singles' group, and we weren't good for that. . . . On any given Sunday you have people who really need to be challenged. But you also have people who are beaten up in ways that you don't even know. You might have people who have had an awful disruption in their lives that week. They really need to know that

the grace of God is there for them, and not just the prophetic words. They need something they can hold on to.

What are worship leaders to do with such diversity in their midst? How can they work faithfully to fashion a worshiping community? One way to deal with diversity in a community is to bow to the centrifugal forces and let everyone go her or his own way, but Christian worship does not work like that. Despite the importance of individual devotional practices, Christians are called to worship corporately, and we do so wherever two or more are gathered together in the name of Jesus Christ. How, then, can worship frames help to bring people together?

Opening worship frames do the complicated work of helping diverse individuals speak with a common voice and communicating to individual worshipers that they are part of a larger community. Through various bracketing strategies, the opening portion of worship gathers together the worshiping body and transforms the varied individuals present into a collective body, a "we." Responsive and unison forms of participation, the content of what is sung or spoken, and the demeanor and conduct of leaders play key roles in the community-building effect of frames.

Tuning In

Let's pick up a point that I stated briefly in the previous chapter: making sound together pulls people into an experience of community. Edward Foley states that "sound events are acts of engagement," because when two or more people hear or produce sound, they interact with each other. Hearing someone else is a personal experience, he says, and it establishes an experience of reciprocity.[6]

Foley goes on to assert that, by virtue of sound's personal and reciprocal nature, singing or speaking in worship unites those present, because it connects those who speak or sing with the listeners, the composer of the music, and the author of the text.[7] The sociologist Alfred Schutz makes the same point about music. When music is performed, he says, performers, listeners, and those who created the music tune in to each other in ways that transcend time and space.[8] In worship the sense of community that can emerge from shared sound making is strongest when people sing or speak in unison. Foley insists that more than any other form, the unison form says "we."[9]

Opening worship frames frequently use responsive and unison forms that encourage people to participate in community-building sound making. For example, the opening frame for the morning service in the *Iona Abbey Worship Book* includes seven elements:

- Opening Responses
- Morning Song of Praise
- Confession
- Silence
- Prayer for God's Help
- Affirmation
- Psalm

All of these worship brackets give people an opportunity to listen and to use their voices—to tune in to each other, as Schutz might say. The opening responses, confession, prayer for God's help, affirmation, and psalm are responsive, with leaders and worshipers alternating their voices. Opportunities for unison participation occur as the congregation sings the morning hymn of praise, observes silence following the confession, and joins in the Lord's Prayer at the conclusion of the prayer for God's help.[10] The opening frame includes all worshipers vocally. People work in harmony with one another and worship as a gathered assembly. They function not only as individuals but also as a collective body, which speaks or sings in a single voice.

This is not to say that all worshipers are on the same page, so to speak, when they participate in an opening frame like this one. The Holy Spirit sometimes sends some people in different directions from others, and worshipers arrive with varied readiness to participate. But I think Foley correctly states that when worshipers act in concert—in song, speech, and silence—there is a sense that they belong to each other and the worshiping body.

Frames also build belonging by their verbal and musical content. Opening frames in many congregations include opportunities for worshipers to greet each other, or for leaders to welcome people to the church. The use of first person plural—"we" or "us"—in songs and prayers reminds people that they have much in common as they worship. Poetic and musical images in various parts of the opening liturgical frame can pull worshipers together into worship and into community.[11]

When liturgical elements are drawn from outside the congregation's dominant culture, poetic and musical images send signals that the church welcomes people from various backgrounds. Singing or speaking images from different cultures also allows a congregation to practice the diversity it preaches. McCormick Theological Seminary strives to be cross-cultural in its life and education. When we worship, we intentionally use liturgical resources that honor the Latino, Asian American, African American, Euro-American, and international cultures in our midst. This is not always easy. Non-Spanish-speakers like me trip over the rapid, lively Spanish in a hymn or response; Westerners struggle with the haunting melodies of Asian hymnody; many fail to catch the subtleties in prayers written from the perspectives of other countries or cultures; people work hard to respect divergent practices regarding gender-inclusive language. But we forge ahead, and as we struggle with various resources, we find that we are stretched as a community. We become bigger, and more faithful, we think, as we expand our worship horizons to be more inclusive. The experience of a variety of faith expressions is not simply a *symbol* of inclusion; it is an *exercise* in inclusion.

Additional bracketing strategies that reflect a congregation's diversity also indicate and exercise a church's openness to the varied backgrounds and tastes of its members. Visual/spatial brackets, such as bulletin art, banners, paraments, and Christian symbols made by people from different artistic traditions welcome, invite, and include diverse populations in worship.

Finally, frames further a sense of belonging when worship is led by people who embody the diversity in the congregation or community. Michael Hawn states that the use of diverse leadership is the most important thing that congregations can do to signal openness to people from varying backgrounds or ethnicity.[12] He describes the effectiveness of using lay leaders as well as clergy in worship's opening brackets, and the importance of using both men

and women in these roles.[13] He argues that congregations wishing
to develop culturally conscious worship and to attract people from
multiple racial and ethnic groups would benefit from reflecting
such diversity in worship leadership. Greeters, too, can be drawn
from a congregation's diversity and give personal and symbolic
welcome to visitors and worshipers.[14]

At the 2006 Presbyterian Association of Musicians conference
at Westminster College in Pennsylvania, every worship service
opened with a procession. Leading each procession was a young
child, seven or eight years old, who wore an alb and carried a glass
pitcher full of water. After all the leaders were in place, the child
carefully poured the water into the font that stood at the front
and center of the chancel, and then took a seat with the congregation. It was wonderful to watch these children lead worship. The
seriousness with which they approached their task, the look of
concentration on their faces as they poured water carefully into
the font, trying not to spill, and their quiet dignity signaled to
everybody that children belonged in that worship service. It was
an added delight at the conclusion of one service to see one small
water bearer, a girl, jump up and down and boldly declare, "I'm
a junior pastor! I'm a junior pastor!" For this girl, taking a role
in leading worship not only affirmed that she belonged to the assembly; it also affirmed that she belonged in the church's ranks of
leadership!

Many congregations indicate their openness to the congregation's diversity by intentionally using bracketing strategies that
welcome people across the social divisions of age, gender, ethnicity, and race, which too often separate human communities and
the church in particular. By recognizing diversity and building it
into the worship frame, congregations indicate that people who
are different from one another all belong together in Christ.

Prayer, Text, and Table

Other dimensions of a worship service also reflect the tension between human limitations and sinfulness on the one hand and the
gracious embrace that God extends to all on the other.[15] In a variety of ways, as worship unfolds, worshipers confront the some-

times uncomfortable truth that God is building a community that
brings together people who would rather stay apart.

I was reminded of this truth many years ago, at a time when
I was making a transition from one call to another. I had just left
a wonderful church, but while I was there some serious conflict
had emerged in the congregation, and some people left the church
angry. I had come to a new city, and on Sunday morning I was en-
joying the opportunity to sit in the pew and worship. As I sat and
reflected, whom should I spot sitting not too far away from me but
one of the couples from my previous church who had left angry
and had refused to speak with me for years? I was not happy; I did
not want to be reminded of that struggle. But as I sat there, I tried
to get a grip on my feelings and realized that this is what it means
to be a member of the body of Christ, whether I liked it or not.
God calls people together across differences, disagreements, and
the workings of our own small minds.[16]

Worship reminds people of the community that God is building among a broken humanity. Prayers lift up the needs of people
far and near, some dear to congregants and others alien to their
culture and way of life.[17] Prayer even intercedes for enemies. Every
time a Christian congregation repeats the Lord's Prayer, people
ask for forgiveness and remind themselves that God invites them
to forgive seventy times seven—far more times than many would
be comfortable with. When worshipers pray, they often experience
the tension between human reality and God's grace.

People experience tension between human sinfulness and God's
grace as they hear multiple texts read and rehearsed in worship.
The presence of more than one text reminds worshipers that the
fullness of God's truth cannot be expressed by only one, limited
voice; many are needed, and even then human expression is insuf-
ficient to say all that could be said. Worship is multivocal, says
Lathrop, and the presence of many voices in worship reminds participants that no single human voice can sufficiently speak God's
truth.[18]

Perhaps the most concrete reminder of the tension that exists
in Christian worship between sinfulness and grace is the table,
where all are invited to remember God's love for humanity in Jesus Christ. Here people are reminded of their limitations as crea-

tures of God, their need for daily bread and renewal, the limits of the earth's resources, and the needs of others. Here, too, they are brought face to face with symbols of God's great blessings.[19] At the table, human limitation and sinfulness stand in tension with God's gracious love for all humankind.

As people worship and experience this tension, worship takes on a remedial nature. Again and again it calls a congregation to be bigger and more generous than its current practice. It reminds people that they do not have the final say on who is welcome; God invites and welcomes all, regardless of their appearance, status, age, need, or capacities.[20]

In worship God builds belonging and forms community. God brings together those who love and care for each other in congregations, and God also pushes against the comfort zones and assumptions of local communities to make them more expansive. God's desire to invite, include, and embrace people is expressed in various ways during a worship service, including song, speech, silence, leadership, prayer, word, and table. Who belongs? We all do, whether we like it or not. Worship teaches us this, and, by God's grace, changes our hearts and minds to welcome it.

Questions for Discussion

1. Which elements of worship in your congregation invite God's people to participate in your faith community, and how is that welcome expressed—in word, style of participation, or symbol?
2. What does your worship service say about who belongs in your congregation?
3. What do you think God would like your worship service to say about belonging?

CHAPTER 5

Frames Articulate Vocation

We may feel that we belong in worship, but to what sort of congregation do we belong? How does our congregation think about itself, or its neighborhood, or its responsibility as part of the body of Christ? How does our congregation live out its faith in the world? I explore questions like these in this chapter, as I extend my discussion of worship frames and their effect on corporate life, with an analysis of how frames express a congregation's vocation.

In the discussion that follows I again focus on boundary and discursive frames. In previous chapters I gave primary attention to the work of boundary frames; but in this chapter I put most emphasis on discursive frames—frames that work through language and metaphor—as I delve into how leaders use sermons and other elements of worship to interpret a congregation's calling.

The Congregation and Its Vocation

Congregations are like human beings. No two are alike, and no two express their faith in exactly the same way. Like any individual Christian, each congregation can be said to have its own vocation. That is, God calls each congregation to live faithfully in a particular time and place, within the constraints of its capacities and perceptions of itself and the world.

Congregational vocations take shape through the interactions of a church with the world around it. Every congregation is involved with the world, whether it wants to be or not, because the boundaries between the congregation and the world are porous. As ethicist H. Richard Niebuhr pointed out more than fifty years ago, even church bodies that think of themselves as living in opposition to the world are unsuccessful at separating themselves completely. Whether the congregation and its world are trying to avoid each other, change each other, or live in a different configuration, there is always movement between the two.[1] For good or ill, the world has an impact on the congregation, and the congregation affects its world.[2] Consequently, one of challenges that falls to clergy and lay leaders is to interpret for current or potential members, other institutions, and strangers how a church relates to its world—its vocation.[3] The interplay of four factors shapes vocational understanding and practice:[4]

- *People:* How a congregation understands its members and the people around them is central to its vocation. Are its members thought of as family members, strangers who gather weekly, an assortment of smaller groups, a holy remnant, or something else? How does the congregation experience the people around it—as neighbors, strangers, allies, enemies, or some combination of these or other categories?

- *Context:* Also important to vocation is how a congregation understands and interprets the world around it. Is the world dangerous or inimical to the church? Is it a benign influence on religious life? Does it support religious life? A church's world includes its cultural, economic, and political contexts, and the congregation's perception of how its context limits its work or opens it to new avenues of mission and service.

- *Theological Orientation:* Every congregation articulates how God calls it to relate to others and to minister in its world. This interpretation makes explicit the sometimes taken-for-granted theological assumptions that churches make when they consider people and contexts, and helps the congregation see how it is called to follow God as an institution set in a particular place and time.

- *Action:* Every congregation ministers through everyday activities that help it bear witness to its faith. These actions are the fourth factor that reflects and shapes a church's vocation.

None of these factors stands alone in a congregation's experience, of course. They inform each other, and it is the interweaving of these self-understandings, contextual interpretation, theological perspective, and action that create the fabric of a church's vocation.

A congregation uses a variety of outlets to interpret its vocation to its members, friends, and others. Church programs, for example, carry implicit messages about a congregation's calling. Vocational interpretation may also be evident on a congregation's website.[5] One of the places this interpretation occurs on a regular basis is in corporate worship.

Worship and Congregational Vocation

Worship is the most important thing a congregation does. In worship the people of the church take time to thank, praise, and commune with God and each other. Here the Holy Spirit gathers people together and nurtures them in faith and discipleship. A church cannot live without genuine, authentic worship. It is at the heart of congregational life, and leaders must approach it with reverence and respect.

At the same time, worship is complex. More occurs in worship than just worship. Families, for instance, nurture their life by worshiping together; congregations pursue stewardship campaigns and recruit volunteers; new friendships sometimes take root. These and other activities need not detract from worship's central purpose, but in some churches they do. Because such a large portion of the congregation's members assemble during worship, sometimes leaders yield to the temptation of using that time to give priority to purposes other than worship, in ways that can overshadow worship. It is important for all leaders to remember how easy it is to abuse the privilege of leading a congregation in adoration, contrition, supplication, and thanks.

I emphasize the importance of worship as worship because for the remainder of this chapter I discuss several ways that congregational vocation is articulated in that setting. I want to be clear that the expression of vocation is a sub-activity in worship. It occurs naturally as leaders pray for the world, interpret Scripture, and suggest how God calls a congregation and its members to express faith; but at the same time it can be abused by leaders who use worship as a platform for other work. Let's all remember that authentic worship, practiced for the sake of God and God's people, should be at the center of our life together in congregations.

How does congregational worship articulate a church's calling? Vocational interpretation arises out of the public nature of worship. Worship is a corporate, public activity, open not only to members of the congregation but also to newcomers and guests. On Sunday morning leaders stand on the boundary between the church and the world, welcome all who choose to attend, and give explicit religious meaning to the work of the congregation. Whether they intend to or not, leaders inevitably send signals in worship about how a congregation views and ministers to the world. In worship, leaders help those present understand what the gospel says and what its implications are for congregational life and mission, as they interpret the Scriptures for their particular place and time, announce opportunities for volunteer service and participation, and welcome newcomers to this assembly.

Worship is one of the first experiences of a congregation that newcomers might have, and it therefore becomes an opportunity for the church to introduce itself to outsiders. When potential members or other visitors encounter a congregation in worship, they get a feel for who the congregation is, how adherents relate to one another, what some of the church programs are, and thus what it stands for. In repeated worship experiences, the contours of the congregation and its vocation become clearer and clearer.

Much of this interpretive work is done by framing. Frame brackets in the gathering and dismissal phases of worship can contribute to a congregation's vocational understanding. Even more powerful are the framing strategies used in other portions of worship, especially sermons.

Bracketing Strategies

The Memorial Day service at the Unitarian Universalist Church I attended had a sturdy, effective worship frame that led and supported me as I worshiped. At the same time, without diluting worship at all, it gave me a good sense of who the congregation is and how it relates to the world. The service began with a recording of chiming bells, the same bells that ring every Sunday morning at the congregation's sister church in Transylvania. As I entered the sanctuary, I noticed the four permanent paintings that lined the chancel wall; on each was a different depiction of a large flame. Along the side of the sanctuary were large windows that allowed worshipers to look out over the church's beautifully landscaped gardens. A lay minister briefly welcomed us to worship, and as he lit the uniquely sculpted chalice lamp, whose replica sits in the congregation's memorial garden, a real flame leapt up, visible to all. He reminded us that it was Memorial Day and invited us to remember those who have given their lives for our country, those who currently serve in the armed forces, and the war on terror. We were quiet as the morning's soloist sang "Hush, Hush, Somebody's Callin' Your Name," and then we sang the opening hymn, which invoked the presence of the "blessed Spirit."

The service continued with actions that characterize many worship services. A child was dedicated. The congregation shared greetings and pastoral concerns. We prayed and listened to a sermon about history, service, and hope. We sang a prayer for peace. We meditated. In a side aisle of the church, many lit votive candles in memory or honor of loved ones.

The service concluded with brackets that sent us forth as peacemakers. We sang a hymn. The lay minister quoted Gandhi and invited us to let his words inspire us to good works. He extinguished the chalice flame. We greeted one another with wishes for peace as the pianist played "Let There Be Peace on Earth."

The worship frame alone gave me a sense of the congregation and its vocation, including its denominational affiliation, social concerns, approach to service, degree of formality, friendliness, and demographics. Program announcements in the bulletin reinforced my perceptions. During the gathering phase of worship, the audible ties to the church in Transylvania suggested that this is a congregation connected to history and its theological tradition, and the use of the Unitarian Universalist hymnal underscored the church's denominational affiliation. Overt yet nonjudgmental discussions of war and peace implied that this church is involved in the world and contemporary issues, but also sensitive to its members, who, I later learned, include both military families and people deeply opposed to the war. The demeanor of the worship leaders and the relative invisibility of the pastor during opening brackets suggested that it is a relatively informal church that welcomes lay leadership. Judging from the appearance of the worshipers, the church is composed predominantly of white, middle-class members of varying ages. Brackets in the gathering and dismissal phases implied that the church believes its members can and should make a difference in the world. It's also a friendly church; warm greetings closed worship, and strangers struck up conversations with me in the coffee hour.

I learned a lot about this church in the gathering and dismissal phases of worship, but a strong worship frame can accomplish this aim. Worship frames can express a congregation's vocation. Brackets are able to communicate how a congregation thinks about itself and others, how it thinks about the world, what sorts of programs and policies and partnerships it pursues, and the theological perspectives that inform this vocation.

Robust worship frames also can signal who a congregation is not. This year Memorial Day Sunday coincided with Pentecost in the Western church calendar, but despite frequent references to "Spirit," there was no mention of the Christian year in this Unitarian Universalist service. Of course, in a UU church, one would expect the absence of trinitarian theology, but Pentecost also marks the birth of the Christian church and has roots in the Jewish Festival of Weeks. Neither of these aspects of Pentecost was mentioned in the service. If I had attended a different UU church that Sunday, one with a stronger Christian orientation, the worship service may well have indicated the congregation's theological orientation with brackets that alluded to or explicitly mentioned the church's birthday. The congregation's decision to skip even a mention of Pentecost distanced it from the more overt Christian orientation that some UU congregations have.

As the illustration above indicates, worship frames sometimes accomplish more than their primary purpose of helping people worship. Effective opening frames can also give members and visitors alike a sense of the church and its vocation. Through words, the demeanor of leaders, cues about denominational affiliation, symbols, and other worship brackets, congregations send signals to people about how they understand and work in the world. Other elements of worship send vocational messages, too, through discursive framing. Sermons are one of the most significant places this signaling occurs.

Discursive Preaching Frames in Two Congregations

If I heard it once over the three years I listened to Elam Davies preach, I heard it a dozen times. As people beloved by God in Christ, we are called as Christians and as a congregation to reach out to "the least, the lost, and the last." From 1962 to 1984, Davies was the pastor of Fourth Presbyterian Church in Chicago, and this was his mantra. Again and again he proclaimed the Christian responsibility for service and charitable outreach to those who most need help. He pursued this agenda in other areas of church life, too, by dismantling programs that privileged the wealthy and initiating multiple ministries of outreach to people who were poor, lonely, or troubled. His preaching legitimated his redirection of the congregation's mission programs, provided a theological rationale for new outreach initiatives, and invited worshipers to adopt new patterns of discipleship through face-to-face service opportunities. During his tenure he repeatedly framed the congregation's vocation as one of compassion, loving others as God loves us.[6]

Davies built this homiletical frame in three ways. First, he consistently interpreted the gospel as a gospel of love. In sermon after sermon, Davies proclaimed the radical, inclusive, sacrificial, embracing love of God for humanity. He had the ability to preach this good news not only in the abstract but also in the particular. It was not uncommon for worshipers in the pews to feel personally embraced by Jesus and his love. Davies's second approach was to use the phrase "the least, the lost, and the last." He invoked this saying often, and he said it enough that congregational leaders could repeat it. It was a short, memorable way to describe the multiplicity and depth of need to which Davies hoped the church would respond more fully. Davies's third approach was to take his time. He built this homiletical frame for more than twenty years; his frame was much more than the work of a single sermon series.[7]

Davies, then, framed the congregation's vocation in this way:

- *People:* We are beloved of God, and our neighbors are those who need God's love and our demonstration of God's love.
- *Context:* The world—especially "the least, the lost, and the last"—needs our help.
- *Theological Orientation:* God loves you with an everlasting love. Love one another as God has loved you.
- *Action:* To respond to God's call, the congregation and individual volunteers engage in ministries of compassion and outreach to people in the immediate neighborhood and surrounding communities (poor children from the housing projects, senior citizens, people needing counseling, patients in the county hospital, prisoners in the county jail, etc.).[8]

Parishioners heard about God's love at the Faith Community of St. Sabina in Chicago, too, but they also heard other messages from the Rev. Michael Pfleger, who framed the Roman Catholic congregation's vocation in distinctive ways appropriate to its neighborhood. A case in point is the way in which Father Pfleger, who is still the pastor at St. Sabina, framed the congregation's participation in church-sponsored, Friday night, anti-drug marches in the 1990s.[9] These marches occurred annually in the summer over many years, and Pfleger's preaching was influential in generating and sustaining involvement.

Pfleger's homiletical approach to framing the congregation's vocation in the context of a neighborhood beset with violence, drugs, homelessness, and alcohol was fourfold. First, he sent a message of possibility. With God's help, Pfleger suggested, the congregation and its members could create neighborhood change. He grounded possibility in the power of God rather than in the power of people themselves. Second, he defined membership in the church as active involvement in the church's programs, including community activism. Sociologist James Cavendish, who analyzed Pfleger's framing, observes that over time people internalized Pfleger's vision of the church as a justice-seeking congregation and his understanding of "the People of God as 'Doers of the Word.'"[10] What it meant to be a member of St. Sabina was to be involved in working for justice in the immediate community. Third, Pfleger encouraged parishioners to consider their involvement in the anti-drug marches as distinctively Christian. They were not only combating the drug trade, he suggested; they were also sowing the word and being evangelists. To march against drugs was to follow Jesus and to bring his love and justice to others. Fourth, like Davies, Pfleger was resilient and consistent in shaping this frame. He reiterated it summer after summer, year after year. And it stuck.

Pfleger thus provided a homiletical frame that helped the congregation to understand its vocation in a particular way:

- *People:* The members of the St. Sabina parish are empowered by God to reach out to people who have been disenfranchised by systemic racism and economic injustice.
- *Context:* The immediate community (the primary focus for ministry in this Roman Catholic parish) is beset by violence, homelessness, drugs, and alcohol. The situation is unacceptable and needs to change.
- *Theological Orientation:* God calls Christians to be doers of the word, not just hearers. Further, because God is on their side, those who follow God faithfully can be successful.
- *Action:* Anti-drug marches and other outreach ministries for social change are appropriate ways for the congregation and individual volunteers to follow God, serve the disenfranchised, and improve neighborhood conditions.

The homiletical frame that Pfleger provided shaped and reshaped the congregation's understanding of its vocation, the meaning of membership, and its actions in the world. When he had first assumed the pastorate there, the congregation's vocation was not as clearly oriented toward justice as it is now. During his ministry he framed and also reframed the congregation's sense of call and level of involvement.[11]

Preaching Frames and Congregational Vocation

These illustrations from Fourth Presbyterian Church and the Faith Community of St. Sabina exemplify how two preachers simultaneously fed their congregations with the gospel and articulated the congregation's vocation in the world. Both Davies and Pfleger coupled preaching with mission initiatives and other pastoral work to lead and redirect the mission of their churches. Through the discursive framing of their sermons, each clearly and consistently provided the theological orientation through which their congregations understood who they were, who their neighbors were, what challenges they faced as a church, and how they could respond to those challenges with faithful ministries. These are examples of effective preaching frames.

Preaching frames fall into the category of what I call discursive frames, and they use language in several ways. Through metaphors, symbols, and other rhetorical strategies, adept preachers can summarize in memorable ways the challenges, theologies, and actions that characterize their congregations' vocations. These metaphors and symbols are often short, terse phrases that call to mind a host of values and concerns.[12] Davies's phrase "the least, the lost, and the last" evokes whole populations of people in need and invites compassion. It also reminds listeners of biblical texts that command compassion. For example, these phrases from two well-known parables come quickly to mind: "Just as you did it to one of the *least* of these . . . you did it to me" (Matt. 25:40, italics added), and "This brother of yours was dead and has come to life; he was *lost* and has been found (Luke 15:32, italics added). Finally, Davies's phrase recalls Jesus's paradoxical statement that "the first shall be *last* and the *last* shall be first" (Matt. 20:16, italics added).

Likewise Pfleger's phrase "Be doers of the word, and not merely hearers" (James 1:22) is a short, biblical quote that is a clear directive; at the same time it reminds hearers of other biblical texts. Psalm 103 promises God's steadfast love and righteousness for those who keep the commandments and "remember to do his covenant" (Ps. 103:18). In Luke 8:21 Jesus tells his followers, "My mother and my brothers are those who hear the word of God and do it." At the conclusion of the parable of the good Samaritan, after Jesus defined a neighbor as one who does mercy, he also tells the lawyer whose question occasioned the parable, "Go and do likewise" (Luke 10:37). The phrase "doers of the word" calls passages like these and others to mind.

Davies was a gifted orator and an effective leader, and Pfleger is an equally eloquent, strong minister. With poetic phrasing or a biblical quotation, their sermons evoke deeply held values and moral frameworks that shape people's actions in the world. Their preaching ministries illustrate how the repeated use of evocative phrases and perspectives can deepen a sense of vocation and commitment in a congregation, especially when coupled with church programming that gives the congregation an outlet to pursue its calling in the world.

Rhetorical flourishes alone, however, cannot account for the efficacy of the preaching frames used by Davies and Pfleger. I do not mean to imply that the only thing that a preacher needs to do to construct a preaching frame is to come up with a pithy phrase and repeat it Sunday after Sunday. Quite the contrary: What made Davies's and Pfleger's frames so effective was a combination of faith, care, and respect for the congregation and its members, along with consistency.

Davies and Pfleger preached from their personal faith and commitment. The values they proclaimed from the pulpit drew directly on biblical narratives and were rooted deeply in each of their hearts. They believed that the work they called the congregation to do was God's work and that it was to be performed for the sake of God and the world God loves. The authenticity of the preachers' faith came through in their framing.

The genuine love and respect that each minister had for the congregation and its members also came through in their preaching. Davies and Pfleger cared for the churches and people they served, and they worked thoughtfully to guide their congregations and members on their respective faith journeys. Their care for their congregations shone through their preaching; their congregations knew they were not being toyed with as they were encouraged to expand their ministries and to take new risks.

Davies and Pfleger also used frames that fit with their congregations. That is, they took into account where the churches had come from, what their capacities for ministry were, the challenges and opportunities in their settings, and the prevailing theology in the congregations' lives; and they worked with what they had. They honored who their churches were, and they gently pushed each church toward what it might become, with God's grace.

Finally, Davies and Pfleger were also consistent with their messages. Their frames were not the work of one or two sermons, but rather were constructed text by text, illustration by illustration, sermon by sermon, as they worked with their congregations to help them be faithful in each one's particular place and time.

Strong preaching frames are discursive strategies that use language creatively to express and shape a congregation's vocation. When rooted in faith and care for the congregation and sensitivity to the congregation's life, and delivered consistently, preaching frames can help a congregation follow God's call to be faithful in the world. Other kinds of discursive frames can articulate a congregation's vocation, too. In some churches, other elements of worship also portray a congregation's vocation and remind worshipers of the work God calls them to do as individuals and as a church.

Signature Symbols and Congregational Vocation

In their study of music in churches and how it expresses and shapes a congregation's life and ministry, church musicians Linda Clark, Joanne Swenson, and Mark Stamm note that many congregations enjoy musical expressions that in some way capture and proclaim who they are as congregations. They call these musical practices "signature symbols."[13] Clark, Swenson, and Stamm use the idea of musical signature symbols to speak of elements of worship that reveal the distinctiveness of a congregation's *piety*—the inner corporate life of a church that is made visible in its programs and practices. I would like to adopt this provocative idea and broaden it to include other practices of worship that are particularly expressive of the congregation's heart and soul—and its vocation. In this broadened sense, then, a signature symbol is a distinctive worship practice that expresses and continues to shape a congregation's vocation. It frames vocation in the context of worship by evoking the particular worldviews, values, and theological convictions that shape the congregation's work in the world. I draw again on a discursive understanding of framing to examine how signature symbols can work.

Distinctive Practices

Many congregations use unique worship practices—signature symbols—that distinguish them from other congregations and remind the church and its members about the particular way a congregation embodies its vocation in the world. The prayer for peace at Lake View Presbyterian Church in Chicago is a case in point.

The prayers of the people at Lake View are divided into three parts. The first two parts occur in the gathering phase of worship, which includes these brackets:

- Musical Prelude
- Opening Hymn
- Prayer for Peace (prayer, part 1)
- Sharing of Joys (members and guests are encouraged to speak up)
- Prayer of Thanksgiving (prayer, part 2)

Toward the conclusion of worship, the congregation solicits prayer concerns from worshipers, prior to a prayer of intercession (part 3). The unusual, three-part arrangement of congregational prayer is a signature symbol at Lake View, but the prayer for peace is a signature symbol all by itself. It sets Lake View apart from other historic mainline Protestant congregations, many of which include joys and concerns in their prayers but do not offer separate prayers for peace on a regular basis. As I write this, I realize that in some churches, particularly those that emphasize peace, like Mennonite, Friends, or Church of the Brethren congregations, separate prayers for peace may not be so unusual, but Lake View's practice is unique among the churches with which I'm most familiar.

Ministries of peace and reconciliation are woven deep into the fabric of Lake View's life. Over the last few decades the church has maintained an alternative high school for school dropouts, provided sanctuary to Salvadoran refugees, supported members who served abroad on Christian peacemaking teams, and openly welcomed gay and lesbian Christians into the church's life. Even when the congregation was so small that it could barely support a pastor and relied on the denomination for extra funding, the congregation supported ministries of peace and justice. These programs and the Christian convictions that shaped and sustained them are evoked every time the Lake View congregation prays for peace. The way this prayer is bracketed by expressions of praise and gratitude symbolically reminds the congregation that its ministries of peace are actions that glorify and thank God.

A very different signature symbol is on display at the House of Hope Presbyterian Church in St. Paul, Minnesota, as worship opens every Sunday.[14] The gathering phase of worship at House of Hope is distinctive. After the prelude, the congregation sings a hymn, during which an elaborate processional ensues. The procession includes the choir, all the pastors, and several acolytes who carry, respectively, the Bible, a cross, a lighted candle taper, and a flag—including the Christian flag and the U.S. flag, and, on some Sundays, the denominational flag and flags that represent countries that nurtured Reformed Christianity (e.g., Scotland and the Netherlands). Banners representing liturgical seasons or symbolizing particular creeds and confessions are sometimes included in the procession. Following the hymn, procession, and lighting of candles, the gathering phase proceeds with opening sentences, the doxology, an invocation, the prayer of confession, a Kyrie, and an assurance of pardon. Throughout the gathering phase, the congregation repeatedly joins in singing liturgical responses.

Although House of Hope's gathering phase does the work that this phase of worship ordinarily does by defining action and focusing attention, it is unique. Not only are the grandeur and elaboration of the procession distinctive, but so is the frequency of congregational song.

Like many other large, regional congregations, House of Hope is a congregation for which worship is of the utmost importance, because it is the aspect of ministry that most consistently brings the congregation together. In addition, House of Hope has an excellent and active ministry of music that includes special worship services, organ and carillon recitals, six choirs, and a choir school. The congregation supports other arts as well. The gathering phase of worship underscores the importance of these ministries at House of Hope. The grandeur and formality of the procession indicate the seriousness with which the congregation takes worship. The frequent recurrence of music and song remind people of the breadth of the music ministry in the congregation.

Other commitments are signaled as well by the gathering phase. I am most impressed with the symbolic force of congregational involvement in the gathering phase. A worshiper cannot participate in the opening brackets of worship at House of Hope without getting the subtle message that her voice and energy are needed in the congregation. Clear yet understated signals of denominational affiliation are sent through the use of *The Presbyterian Hymnal* (1990) and the denomination's flag.

A worshiper at House of Hope Presbyterian Church knows where she is. She is worshiping in a Presbyterian church that is deeply committed to worship, the ministry of music and the arts, and its members' participation in worship and other ministries. The gathering phase outlines the contours of the congregation's vocation. It is a signature symbol.

In chapter 3 signature symbols from two other congregations were described. The sung offertory response in my congregation and the closing song at Grace, about which Hawn writes, are practices unique to these congregations, which express and reinforce these congregations' vocations.[15] My congregation tends to have a civic stance that empowers individuals to live faithfully in the world and to serve God wherever they might find themselves.[16] Grace seeks to embrace diversity and to welcome people into Christian unity and fellowship. The songs that each congregation sings clearly express these orientations.

Many congregations employ distinctive worship practices that symbolize their vocational stance in the world. As these examples indicate, sometimes these symbols are regular practices that the congregation observes almost weekly. In other congregations, however, signature symbols take the form of annual worship services that express the congregation's vocation.

Special Worship Services

In their discussion of the Maundy Thursday Tenebrae service at one of the congregations they studied, Clark, Swenson, and Stamm illustrate how an annual worship practice can be a signature symbol. They contend that this service is an annual expression of the congregation's deepest piety, and that it in turn continues to shape that piety.[17] In like manner, annual worship services in other congregations can express and shape a congregation's vocation.

Southminster Presbyterian Church loves the annual festival of mission and hymnody that it observes every January. Using the format of lessons and carols as a template, the congregation hears stories about God's work in the world and intersperses those stories with hymns and prayers. The stories are told by representatives from local agencies and congregations that Southminster supports with its mission dollars and volunteers. In 2001, when I was observing and participating in worship at Southminster, the church heard about ministries that strengthen spiritual life, empower children, rehabilitate housing, support people in drug rehabilitation programs, and help homeless people find housing on Chicago's North Side. It heard also from the pastor of a new Latino church development in a Chicago suburb, and it received thanks from two seminarians whose studies it was supporting.

A service like this one reminds Southminster of its partners in ministry, through and with whom the congregation is able to embody its vocation. One of the significant ways this congregation reaches out in mission is through these partnerships. Representatives from these ministries gave voice to the congregation's understanding of its work in the world. This service is a signature symbol for Southminster.

A very different sort of service is a signature symbol for the First Presbyterian Church of Hartford, Connecticut, where the annual Founders' Day celebration is the worship and coffee-hour highlight of the year. I served as the pastor of this church from 1991 to 1995 and can attest to the importance of this service.

Everything comes together on Founders' Day, which is always celebrated on the first Sunday of November. During this service the church receives new members, baptizes children, honors fifty-year and fifty-year-plus members, prays for members who have died in the past year, and shares the sacrament of communion. On Founders' Day the congregation remembers where it has been and tries to articulate where it is going. New and old come together. Families worship together; some remember great-grandparents who were founding members of the congregation, and others remember significant contributions that their parents or other relatives made to the church across the years. It is a homecoming, a gathering of the church's people and history and a restatement of its vocation.

The real highlight of the morning is not the worship service but the coffee hour that comes afterward.[18] The silver has all been polished. Women bring desserts worth standing in line for, and the shortbread base in many of these desserts reminds people of the congregation's strong Scottish heritage. Here the genuine ties of family and friendship are expressed and reinforced in the enjoyment of food, refreshment, and each other.

The vocation of First Presbyterian Church is deeply rooted in its history. Its abiding commitment to serving its members, nurturing a deeply intertwined network of relationships, and honoring simple dedication to faithful discipleship are 150-year-old values and practices that are expressed repeatedly in the congregation's work. That comes through loud and clear on Founders' Day, when the church celebrates who it has been and who God might be calling it to be.

By embodying a congregation's deepest values and giving expression to the distinctive way a congregation engages the world, signature symbols in worship contribute to framing a congregation's vocation. Because they are symbols rather than more elaborately constructed rhetorical arguments such as worshipers might hear in a sermon, signature symbols do not always explicitly interpret a congregation's vocation. Rather, they capture and express it in the practice of worship in a variety of ways. A prayer for peace, a unique gathering phase, a closing song, an annual celebration of mission, the annual church family reunion—all are moments of worship that locate worshipers in that particular congregation and indicate something of how the congregation tends to engage the world.

Certainly other elements of congregational life give voice to the congregation's vocation, too. But the nature of worship demands that it bear significant responsibility for presenting the public face of the congregation. Worship is often the first point of contact for visitors and the most customary point of contact for occasional attenders. Worship occurs with dependable regularity. And worship is the place where believers strain to hear the word and will of God. While it is not an occasion to be manipulated for other purposes, it is nonetheless a time when congregational leaders interpret God's call in light of the world's challenges, and help their churches understand how they can serve God faithfully. In many cases, it is boundary or discursive framing that leaders use to help them do this interpretive work.

Questions for Discussion

1. How would you characterize your congregation's vocation?
2. What theological convictions shape your church's engagement with the world?
3. How (if at all) do the boundary or discursive frames of your worship service express what you believe God calls your church to be and do?

CHAPTER 6

Frames, Worship, and Change

In the previous chapters I mentioned the idea of "reframing" more than once, and here I take it up in earnest with a discussion of how leaders can change worship frames, and the effect that frame change can have on a congregation's worship and ministry. Because knowing how to modify frames can be such a useful tool for ministry, it is worth taking time to consider how frame change occurs.

Reframing: Four Approaches

Central to any understanding of frames is the awareness that frames are not static. Frames can be transformed by both accident and intent, and frame change can occur in various ways.[1] The four approaches to frame analysis, which are reviewed in chapter 1, view reframing processes differently. Below I outline the distinctions between the four, and give particular attention to boundary and discursive frame change. Because congregational leaders are likely to be familiar with problem definition and solution frames and perspective frames, I also describe the ideas about reframing that characterize them.

Changing Boundary Frames

Boundary frames are constructed by combining a series of brackets in ways that define action. In chapter 1, I used the TV show *Mr.*

Rogers' Neighborhood to illustrate how boundary frames work. On that show Mr. Rogers combined his entrance, change of clothing, and song to make children feel welcome and set the stage for the next half-hour, during which he shared his neighborhood with viewers. Mr. Rogers closed the frame by reversing the actions that had opened the show. The particular brackets and the way they were combined constituted the frame.

Leaders can change boundary frames by rearranging, amending, adding, or subtracting brackets.[2] Many years ago on *Saturday Night Live*, the comedian Eddie Murphy changed Mr. Rogers' frame to spoof the children's show with skits titled "Mr. Robinson's Neighborhood." In those skits, Murphy did the same things that Mr. Rogers did—he entered the living room, changed into his sweater and different shoes, and introduced himself. But when Murphy added a bracket, like showing viewers the bag of groceries that he said he had just snatched from an old lady on the street, viewers quickly knew that they were in a very different neighborhood from the one that children visited with Mr. Rogers. The addition of the "stolen" groceries, the change of actors, the attitude with which the actor performed, and the comedic setting of *Saturday Night Live* were bracket changes that reframed what viewers saw.

We see boundary reframing all the time on TV comedy. *The Daily Show* and *The Colbert Report*, fake news shows on Comedy Central, satirize the news media with subtle frame changes. Comedians replace journalists in the anchor seat—a key bracket change—and the additional bracket changes marked by differences in their demeanor, the news with which they choose to open their shows, and their comments on the news indicate that viewers are seeing something other than an ordinary newscast. Despite the fact that many young adults claim to get their news from these TV shows, everybody knows that these shows are comedy, not news. Reframing changes the experience that viewers have, from watching news to watching comedy, and changes in content throughout the shows intensify the frame change.

A nonverbal example of boundary frame change is the chrome fish found on the back of many automobiles. Some of the fish are simply two curved lines joined together to form the shape of a fish with a tail. These simple drawings evoke stories of how early

Christians identified themselves to one another and suggest that the owners of the car are Christians. The fish image frames our understanding of the person who owns that car. What happens when someone adds brackets to one of those fish—say, two feet and the name "Darwin"? The Darwin fish no longer makes a Christian claim; it makes a political statement in opposition to some faith claims, and the new frame leads us to assume that the same faith-opposing, political stance characterizes that car's owners. When a third bracket is added to the Darwin fish, and a fish labeled "Truth" eats one labeled "Darwin," the chrome-fish argument is taken one step further, and so is our understanding of the frame statement it makes. The simple addition or subtraction of brackets can entirely change the meaning of the frame.

Many worship leaders already know how to change boundary frames, because they do it often as they adapt worship services to make seasonal or style changes. I discuss reframing and worship styles in more detail below.

Changing Discursive Frames

Scholars who approach frames as discourse speak of frames as mental constructs that express shared values and shape our perspectives and actions. These mental constructs are normally expressed through metaphors, symbols, or words and phrases that evoke a particular worldview.[3]

Leaders change discursive frames with the use of new language that brings different values or worldviews to the fore. Examples of discursive reframing abound. When Gandhi evoked deeply held, cherished British values as he argued for Indian independence, he reframed the independence movement by juxtaposing the old British values with the Indian desire for freedom, and effectively changed the movement from a revolt against British values to one that embodied them.[4] When President George W. Bush charged that Democrats who opposed the war in Iraq wanted to "cut and run," his use of that phrase undermined their arguments and put them on the defensive; it reframed the discussion and put the values that he wanted to promote at the center of the debate. In chapter 1, I described the effectiveness of the frame "pro-life" in the anti-abortion movement. That phrase reframed the abortion discussion by shifting the focus of the conflict from reproductive freedom to the life of the unborn. Discursive frames get reframed when leaders find new, effective language to express or highlight the values they seek to promote.[5]

Discursive framing and reframing need not occur only in conflicted situations, like the examples I used above. Leaders can use discursive frames in all sorts of situations. Below I discuss two examples of preachers who used reframing in their preaching to reshape their congregation's vocation.

Changing Problem Definition and Resolution Frames

In chapter 1, I illustrated the problem definition and resolution approach to frame analysis with the example of a mother whose child cried in the church nursery on Sunday morning. The mother's first response to the crying was to spend time calming the child, but it was an ineffective response and in fact made the situation worse. A different response—the mother's leaving the nursery almost immediately while the child was still in tears—seemed to be more effective; the child calmed down more quickly, and the mother was able to attend worship.

Reframing occurred in this situation when the situation was defined differently, and the mother's ineffective behavior became the focus for resolving the problem; changing her behavior made all the difference. When frame analysis is approached as problem definition and solution, the approach to reframing is usually applicable in situations like this illustration, in which there seems to be an unending cycle of troubling behavior and inappropriate response. The situation is reframed by redefining the problem and focusing change efforts not on the presenting symptoms (the child's crying) but rather on the failed solution (the mother's attempts at comfort).[6]

Changing Perspective Frames

In the world of organization development, a frame is a perspective from which to view and direct behavior and processes in organizations. In their work on frames and reframing, Bolman and

Deal identify four frames that organization development scholars use to analyze life in organizations and institutions: structural, human behavioral, political, and symbolic. They contend that many leaders tend to gravitate to one frame, and that a single-frame approach limits leaders' capacity to work effectively in an organization. They therefore encourage leaders to move outside their frame comfort zones, understand the differences among frame perspectives, move knowledgeably from one to the other, and make use of more than one frame at a time when addressing issues in organizations. Reframing in this approach, then, is shifting between frames or using multiple frames at once, instead of getting stuck in just one.[7]

Although congregational leaders may wish to employ various approaches to reframing in their work, when it comes to worship, boundary frames and discursive frames are, I think, the frames that leaders use most prevalently. In the discussion that follows, I illustrate how leaders have reframed worship and congregational life using both kinds of frames.

Reframing Worship Boundaries

Reframing can be used to change worship in a congregation, and modifying worship brackets is one of the quickest ways to make this happen. An example of the difference that bracket changes can bring to worship is the practice of using an Advent wreath during the four Sundays preceding Christmas. In many congregations the lighting of the Advent wreath and the accompanying liturgy are brackets added to the gathering phase of worship. The addition of this practice at the beginning of worship, along with shifts in music and liturgical colors, reframes the liturgical season from ordinary time to a season of fasting and waiting, and helps worshipers make the transition to Advent.[8]

A more dramatic example of how boundary reframing can alter worship is the frame modifications that many congregations made to shift from traditional to contemporary worship. To initiate this change in worship, congregational leaders reframed worship by making some or all of the following bracket changes in the gathering phase of worship:

- Replaced the organ with an amplified praise band (piano, guitars, drums, and/or other instruments).
- Replaced hymnody with praise-and-worship music (and replaced hymnals with presentation software and projection screens).
- Replaced the choir with a praise-and-worship team.
- Eliminated the wearing of pastoral robes or vestments.
- Eliminated the procession of leaders or made it less formal.
- Eliminated or lessened the use of chancel furnishings or space.
- Eliminated or lessened the use of traditional liturgical forms to open worship, such as a call to worship or invocation.
- Where possible, reconfigured congregational seating to modify the cathedral pattern that characterizes many worship spaces.

People often discuss traditional and contemporary worship in a way that suggests that the primary differences between the two are the resources that people use in worship, such as hymns or praise-and-worship music.[9] I disagree. Although resource selection can profoundly shape worship, the bundle of resources, actions, and configurations that combine to make a worship frame has even more impact. It is the frame of worship about which people argue in the traditional-or-contemporary worship wars, not individual resources alone.

Every one of the changes listed above involves more than a resource change. Each is a bracket change, and when a congregation makes such changes, it restructures the gathering phase of worship. It creates a new frame, which, as I discussed earlier, modifies how the gathering phase establishes action in worship—the style of invitation, degree of formality, and emotion norms.

At Southminster Presbyterian Church, whose contemporary worship service I discussed in chapters 2 and 3, the congregation also has a traditional worship service on Sunday mornings. To make a clear distinction between the two services, the leaders built different opening frames. The traditional service opens with an organ prelude and a stately procession that includes the choir, the pastor, the lay leader carrying a large Bible that she solemnly opens and places on the communion table, and an acolyte carrying a lighted candle taper, with which she lights the candles. A choral introit, the opening hymn, a unison prayer of confession, a time of silence, the Kyrie sung in unison, and the assurance of pardon follow. The frame—the combined effect of all these worship brackets—establishes action that is formal in demeanor, reserved in emotional tone, and visibly Presbyterian in its use of resources and order of worship.

Southminster's contemporary worship service uses a different frame. After the leaders set up the worship space, rehearse, and gather for worship—there is no official procession—a piano prelude begins worship. Greetings and congregational singing, led by the praise-and-worship team, follow the prelude, and the congregation concludes the gathering phase as the lay leader reads a psalm and the pastor offers a prayer of confession and assurance of pardon on the congregation's behalf. The opening frame of this service is quite different from the one the congregation uses in its traditional service. The frame establishes action that is more informal and an emotional tone of excitement and joy, and it downplays the Presbyterian identity of the congregation.

Leaders at Southminster intentionally changed the worship frame of the second service to make it different from the earlier service. In their efforts to reach out to more people in their community and to offer members two options for worship, they created services that provided people distinctly different choices on Sunday morning. The alternatives they developed are shaped almost entirely by boundary-framing strategies. Little difference exists between the opening and closing frames of the two services, although the contemporary service includes fewer Scripture readings and eliminates the Apostles' Creed. In most other ways, the services are identical: the same children's message and sermon are preached, the style and substance of prayers are the same, and other elements of worship like the offering are similar, too. What distinguishes the services from each other and shapes worshipers' experiences quite differently are the distinct worship frames. And these frames are effective; they result in two services that worshipers feel are quite different from each other.

What results from both frames is still worship, of course, and the contemporary and traditional frames can be equally effective in pulling worshipers together in the presence of God to apprehend God's love and guidance. But the two styles vary in their approach to worship work, and their distinct frames shape those divergent approaches.

Another example of how leaders reframe worship boundaries is the changes that some congregations have made to create services that are more multicultural. In their book *People of the Dream*, sociologist Michael Emerson and pastor Rodney Woo assert that a charismatic worship style correlates with higher racial diversity in congregations.[10] To illustrate the difference that worship can make for congregations that want to embrace such diversity, they document the changes that Wilcrest Baptist Church in Houston, Texas, made to help the congregation embody its vision of being multiracial. Among the alterations that the church made to accomplish its dream were changes in the worship frame that included the development of a new congregational logo and motto ("Love in Any Language") that was displayed in the narthex and printed on the cover of the worship bulletin; the addition of conga drums and a bass guitar to the instrumentation for worship music; the diversification of the choir, which became multiracial; and the designation of worship leaders who represented the racial diversity of the congregation and its neighborhood. Emerson and Woo discuss how worship frame changes resulted in services that were more emotionally expressive than previous services, and they indicate that members noticed the increased volume and livelier pace of the worship music. The frame change in worship attracted new members, satisfied many older members, and unfortunately impelled some members to find new church homes because the worship changes did not feel "right" to them.[11]

When boundary frames change to make worship more multicultural, the modifications redefine the action of worship. The invitation offered in worship broadens by extending implicit and explicit welcome to people from more than one race, ethnicity, or generation. Sometimes the degree of formality changes too, or the emotion norms that worship employs. Reframing worship boundaries establishes new action.

Sometimes worship reframing changes more than worship; it can also modify the theological perspective of a congregation. In his study of nine Lutheran congregations in the Pacific Northwest, sociologist Stephen Ellingson analyzes worship frame change in several of the churches that shifted from a traditional Lutheran pattern of worship to a style of worship more characteristic of evangelical churches. He demonstrates that not only did worship reframing alter worship; in addition, new worship brackets, coupled with shifts in discursive framing, changed the basic theological orientations of these congregations. They became less distinctly Lutheran, less reflective of the historic Protestant mainline, and more evangelical in their theological outlooks than previously. Reframing worship helped to create these changes.[12]

Congregational leaders can change worship by removing, adding, or modifying brackets in the gathering and dismissal phases of worship. But before they rush headlong into reframing worship, it is wise for leaders to consider how easy it is to upset people with changes in the gathering phase of worship. The gathering phase—the opening frame—sets everything up. It gets participants ready for whatever is about to come, invites people, and establishes the tone for worship. Because opening frames carry the weight of action definition, when changes are made in opening frames, people notice it more and feel its effects more strongly than they do changes in any other part of worship. Why? Because changes in the gathering phase of worship redefine the action.

Frame Change and Conflict

Reframing worship boundaries in the gathering phase can, therefore, be controversial.[13] We should not be surprised, then, as we look back at the contemporary-vs.-traditional worship wars that many congregations endured, by how intense these worship fights were. People were not just fighting about whether or not to sing hymns or wear robes. They were fighting about fundamental variations in frames that established different action: new styles of invitation, degrees of formality, emotion norms, and, in some places, theological perspectives.

Less controversial changes in worship can be accomplished when leaders make changes in the core of a worship service rather than in the opening or closing frames. Because changes in the middle of a worship structure do not disrupt the boundary frame, they may be easier to implement, depending on how radical or extensive they are. The reason that they are easier to implement is that changes to the boundary frame reconfigure action, whereas changes in the middle of a worship service do not necessarily shift the action in such fundamental ways.

For example, I watch with interest a pastor who serves a redeveloping congregation and is trying to help the congregation make its worship more multi-sensory. The pastor has introduced video and drama to the congregation as part of its worship, but she has done so without breaking the worship frame to which the congregation is accustomed. Instead, she plays with the form and shape of the sermon. Although she preaches in a rather traditional form, she occasionally experiments and pushes the envelope of Scripture reading and preaching with video clips, drama, or projected images. The congregation enjoys these variations. Granted, this is a flexible and forward-looking congregation, but many of its members are traditional in heritage and outlook, and they are comfortable with their tradition. I am impressed that this pastor has been able to introduce new technology and approaches to worship with so little disruption. I think she has been successful partly because she has worked from the inside out. Once the congregation is comfortable with some of the newer forms, she can introduce them in other parts of the worship service—maybe even the opening brackets. In fact, she has used video clips during opening brackets on occasion but has not made this a permanent addition to the service.

Leaders who want to experiment with new worship practices can introduce them more easily if they introduce new practices outside the opening frame—in portions of the service other than the gathering phase. Remember, the opening frame establishes action; changes here modify worship's action and are usually more disruptive for people than are changes in other parts of worship, because they are more noticeable. Why not experiment with less disruption rather than more, and introduce new practices after the gathering phase is finished? Once people have, with repetition, gained some competence and comfort with the new resources, then the use of those resources can be expanded and maybe even introduced into the opening frame. Handling worship change in this way, from the core to the frame, will likely be less jarring for people than beginning with frame change.

Worship Frames, Change, and Congregational Vocation

Worship frames can express and shape a congregation's vocation. Boundary frames send strong signals about a congregation's priorities and values; discursive preaching frames interpret and inspire how a congregation understands its calling; and signature symbols embody the style and commitments of a church. Not every congregation, of course, chooses to use worship frames in this way, but those that do find that worship frames complement and promote the congregation's calling.

Neither worship frames nor congregational vocations are carved in stone, however; both can and do change over time. Changes in congregational vocation are affected by shifts in one or more of the four variables that constitute it: people, context, theological orientation, and action. Because how a congregation understands itself and its neighbors, its location, the gospel, and its mission is often expressed in a multiplicity of worship elements, worship is a central arena in which a congregation's values, purpose, perspectives, and understandings are both expressed and shaped. As aspects of a congregation's reality shift, whether by intention or accident, worship provides an occasion for interpretation and reinterpretation—in a word, reframing.

Changes in boundary worship frames are created by modifying the brackets, and, in some cases, that change can express the evolution of a congregation's vocation. The example above of Wilcrest Baptist Church is a case in point. When the church altered its opening frame from one that used Euro-American hymns and liturgies to one that used liturgical elements from African, Caribbean, and Latino Christian traditions, the reframing gave expression to the congregation's determination to be more racially inclusive. The congregation's convictions resulted from its new understanding of its vocation. It had redefined its understanding of itself (changing from satisfaction to dissatisfaction with its previous mono-racial composition), its neighbors (from outsiders to potential members and friends), and its theology and actions (developing a multiracial church as a witness to the gospel). These new convictions were expressed by the congregation in many ways, including its worship frames.[14]

Preaching Frames

Changes in discursive frames can occur in a number of ways. Social movement theorists Robert Benford and David Snow have done extensive analyses of discursive framing in various social movements. One of the aspects of framing that they examine is how speech can be used to develop, elaborate, or change frames. They identify strategies that leaders use to reconfigure frames, two of which are relevant for this discussion:[15]

- Frame transformation is a fundamental change that alters old understandings and generates new ones. Benford and Snow indicate that few studies exist about frame transformation, but state that an example is the success of feminist efforts to reframe the public's understanding of rape, from understandings shaped by racist and sexist misconceptions that tended to blame the victim, to perceptions of rape as a serious crime.
- Frame extension broadens a group's interests to include new concerns that are considered to be important to potential adherents. The evolution of the gay-lesbian movement illustrates frame extension. The movement first focused on gay rights, and then broadened to include lesbian rights; later the rights of bisexual and transgender persons were embraced by the movement. The frame expanded over time to include a wider variety of people and experiences.[16]

As a congregation's vocation shifts, preachers can use any of the strategies identified by Benford and Snow to reframe a congregation's understanding of its vocation. By making use of the rhetorical space and the weekly opportunity that preaching provides, a pastor can articulate a church's changing understanding of itself, the people around it, its context, and its programmatic ministry. The following examples illustrate how sermons can support and shape a congregation's vocation. Both are drawn from published collections of sermons, one by the Rev. John Fry, former pastor of First Presbyterian Church in Chicago, who uses a frame transformation strategy, and another by the Rev. Dr. Jeremiah Wright, pastor emeritus of Trinity United Church of Christ in Chicago, who uses a frame extension strategy.[17] In both of these illustrations, preaching contributes to vocational reframing through discourse.

First Presbyterian Church in Chicago

In the 1950s and 1960s the Woodlawn neighborhood on Chicago's South Side underwent significant population and economic changes. The neighborhood was quickly transformed from white to black and from middle class to working class or underclass. Businesses left or failed; homes were abandoned. Gang activity, arson, and other forms of violence characterized the neighborhood.

The neighborhood had been quite different when First Presbyterian Church moved there in the 1920s. The white, middle-class neighborhood of the earlier decades supported the congregation, and in 1949 the church reached its membership peak of more than two thousand adherents. Rapid racial succession and economic decline in the neighborhood, however, took their toll on the congregation, and its membership declined, too. The church had to make a decision: stay or relocate. Although the move in the 1920s had been driven by a desire to move to a segregated neighborhood, in 1952 the congregation decided to stay in Woodlawn, integrate the membership, and serve the neighborhood. To facilitate these commitments, the church hired an integrated co-pastor team in 1956.[18]

The significant changes in the demographics of the congregation and its neighborhood, the economy, and level of safety in the community forced First Presbyterian Church to re-examine its vocation. The church had shrunk in membership, its neighborhood had changed from Caucasian to African American, and the neighborhood was less stable than it once was. The church believed

that it had to reorient its vocation to be faithful. The leaders decided to become more active in the community; the congregation
joined with three other churches, and in 1960 the four congregations worked with community organizer Saul Alinsky to form the
Woodlawn Organization. Other community initiatives were begun
as well.[19]

By 1960, then, the congregation had three legs of a new vocation in place: new people and neighbors, a changed context, and a
new action plan. All that was needed was a strong theological orientation to support and nurture the congregation's new approaches to ministry. Undoubtedly the co-pastors in the 1950s and '60s
worked diligently to articulate a theological interpretation of the
congregation's new calling and work. So did the pastor who suc-
ceeded them, a man named John Fry. A number of Fry's sermons
from this time have been collected and published, and the collection demonstrates how one pastor used preaching to reframe and
interpret the congregation's vocation and approach to the world.[20]
Because the church was undergoing such a radical change in its
vocation, the sermons exemplify frame transformation.

In a speech at a congregational meeting, Fry articulated the
theology that shaped his ministry at First. He identified four convictions: (1) The church is a missionary agency whose purpose is
to give its life away; (2) the church is called to identify with its
neighbors and, when appropriate, to lift up their hopes for the
future; (3) the church at its best represents hope and upholds a
messianic vision of humane relationships in a humane city; and (4)
the church is called to uphold the humanity of black human
beings.[21]

These convictions shaped Fry's preaching, and in sermon after
sermon he forged a frame that articulated the congregation's vocation and responsibility. He reminded the church of the desperation
of the powerless, many of whom were neighborhood residents.
He described the presence and depths of systemic racism and injustice in Woodlawn, Chicago, and the United States. Finally, he
proclaimed God's power to deliver and redeem, despite all appear-
ances of hopelessness or defeat.

The Scripture texts on which Fry preached often were texts of
confrontation. They depicted Jesus or another divine agent coming

face to face with human suffering or injustice—and bringing deliverance. Fry reminded his listeners and readers that in the presence of God the blind receive sight, the sick are healed, and the priests of Baal are rendered impotent. God wills deliverance. God wills redemption. God wills the breaking of sin and death. Such preaching reminded people that they were not alone in their own struggles or confrontations and that the work of redemption, however incomplete it might be at a human level, is the work of God.

Fry's sermons exemplify how preaching can support a congregation as it walks a new, difficult path in the world. The sermons were consistently oriented toward the redemptive work that Fry and the congregation's leaders believed First Presbyterian was called to do. Fry was honest about the evil he saw, yet the hope he continued to offer was grounded in the biblical witness and his faith. He offered the congregation a theological orientation that was consistent with the needs of the people, the realities of the context, and the congregation's action. In so doing, he used preaching to reframe the congregation's work in ways that helped the church live into its new calling.[22]

Fry's sermons are good examples of frame transformation. His homiletical frame expressed the radical change that the congregation's vocation had already undergone. Fry's preaching gave theological justification for the work that arose from the congregation's changed circumstances and its new commitments to ministry in Woodlawn.

Trinity United Church of Christ in Chicago

Not every vocational shift requires the drastic reframing that sends congregations like First Presbyterian in entirely new directions. Some reframing starts with a solid frame and expands it—what Benford and Snow would call frame extension. Some of the Rev. Jeremiah Wright's preaching illustrates this approach to reframing.

Shortly before Wright became the pastor of Trinity UCC, the congregation adopted a new motto to fit its changing sense of vocation: "Unashamedly Black and Unapologetically Christian." Since the early 1970s the congregation has lived into this motto, affirmed its trust in God, and developed a multidimensional ministry to the black community.[23] Wright's preaching has been instrumental in guiding and nurturing the congregation's growth and adherence to its vocation, which is shaped by its membership; the needs of black communities in Trinity's immediate neighborhood, the United States, and overseas; the church's understanding of the racialized context in which it ministers; and the congregation's faith and ministries.

Several years ago Wright preached a series of sermons on the family that delivered several messages.[24] In some of the sermons Wright talked about family life in ways that fit the norms of family life that tend to prevail in the United States—the norms of nuclear families with two parents and a couple of children. In these sermons Wright offered support to family members who were working hard to be loving and responsible in their roles as parents, spouses, and children. In other sermons he challenged those who fell short of their responsibilities and invited them to repentance. "You don't have to end up like you started out. Jesus can change the ending of your story,"[25] he once proclaimed. These sermons challenged neither Trinity's vocation nor the wider cultural norms of family life.

Other sermons in this collection, however, sought to expand Trinity's sense of vocation and challenged prevailing cultural understandings of family life. In these sermons Wright tried to reframe worshipers' understanding of the family to be more inclusive of families who may not fit common cultural norms—single-parent families, blended families, and couples in same-sex relationships. Wright announced, "Those whom the righteous can't stand to be around, God can't stand to be without."[26]

In the sermons that discussed unconventional family arrangements, Wright juxtaposed contemporary family life, which is often unconventional, with two kinds of texts: those that proclaim the unconditional love of God and biblical narratives of families that did not fit the norm of their day either. His juxtaposition of contemporary situations with messages of God's love and biblical narratives about unconventional families broadened worshipers' understanding of family and God's presence in family life. These juxtapositions also offered a countercultural challenge to the narrower definitions of family that some in the wider culture promote.

Wright's sermon series both honored and modified Trinity's vocation. The sermons were consistent with Trinity's commitment to uphold black people as they try to live faithfully in a racialized and racist society. Wright was honest and realistic about the challenges people face and the burdens they carry. He was also honest about everyday human sinfulness and did not hesitate to challenge it. These sermons addressed vital pastoral concerns and lifted people up with messages of faith, forgiveness, and hope; and they honored Trinity's vocation. At the same time, in some sermons Wright gently pushed the envelope of Trinity's vocation by challenging people to think differently about themselves, their neighbors, and the gospel. That is, he tried to stretch Trinity's understanding of its members, neighbors, and social context. He insisted that God's acceptance and forgiving love have already embraced families who might appear to be unconventional, and suggested that Trinity's call is to follow where God has already gone.

Although these sermons laid down a challenge to the congregation, in them Wright did not fundamentally redirect Trinity's vocation. He instead tried to make that vocation bigger by affirming the unconventional families in the congregation and the larger community, and reminding worshipers of God's radical love in Jesus Christ. Wright used a strategy of frame extension to do this. With his sermons he implied that Trinity's membership and mission could include all sorts of families, not just ones that looked healthy on the outside because they fit into conventional family norms. He implied that the church could have a bigger heart, a bigger reach when it came to families, and that becoming more inclusive of alternative family structures and experiences would make the congregation more Christlike.

Both Fry and Wright engaged in preaching that framed and reframed their congregations' vocations, although neither made use of the types of brief, metaphorical phrases or symbols that preachers like Davies and Pfleger used repeatedly in their sermons. Instead, Fry and Wright used the force of biblical narrative to evoke the values and worldviews they encouraged their congregations to embrace. The frames they constructed resonated with their deep faith in God's liberating presence in human life and God's unwavering commitment to people whom others may judge as aberrant.

Vocational Change and Other Elements of Worship

Other elements of worship can, of course, reinforce the changing definition of vocation in a congregation. As noted earlier, the introduction of new music or worship leaders can represent the changing demographics of a congregation or its neighborhood. The content of prayers can offer new interpretations of a congregation's context or speak a fresh theological vision. Announcements and "minutes for mission" can highlight new action initiatives and invite worshipers' participation. Numerous elements of worship can be used responsibly to lift up changes in a congregation's understandings of people, context, theology, or action, and thus forward changes in the church's sense of vocation.

Worship Frames and Change

"My congregation refuses to change," say many pastors and church leaders. I doubt that is true of most churches, because congregations change all the time, whether their members like it or not. People come and go; cultural shifts affect congregational life and worshipers' attitudes; leadership turns over; new theological insights offer fresh perspectives. Congregations are in constant flux.

As congregations change, sometimes their worship frames change, too. This chapter has illustrated some ways that can happen. When a congregation adopts new worship styles, the changes that result sometimes create a fundamental frame change through the simultaneous realignment of several worship brackets. Gentler frame changes can be instituted by adding or subtracting fewer brackets, or by introducing change toward the middle of the service and letting worshipers adjust more slowly. Preaching frames can be powerful, too, as ministers use sermons to articulate vocational shifts that realign or expand a church's ministry.

Not all frame changes are as intentional or as well conceived as others. But when a congregation and its leaders consider frame change carefully and make thoughtful, appropriate shifts in worship frames, such changes can enhance a church's ministry and clarify its sense of vocation.

Questions for Discussion

1. How has your congregation changed over the years?
2. As your church has adjusted to changes in people, context, theology, or programs, how have those changes been expressed or shaped in worship?
3. How does worship nurture and support your congregation, its members, and its mission?

CHAPTER 7

Strengthening Worship Frames

Frame change does not always need to be as big or dramatic as the changes I discussed in chapter 6. Sometimes congregations want to modify frames gently to improve worship—to amplify the invitational aspect of the opening frame, for example, or to lift up the significance of a sacrament. What steps can leaders take when they want to strengthen a good frame that's already in place?

I encountered this challenge in the 1990s when I was the pastor at the First Presbyterian Church in Hartford, Connecticut. The choir and its leadership played a significant role in the opening worship frame at First Presbyterian. Worship opened with an organ prelude followed by a choral introit sung in the narthex. After a responsive call to worship, the choir led the opening hymn as it entered in procession down the center aisle and choir members took their places in the loft behind the central pulpit. The choir's presence was important. Not only did the choral introit complement the prelude and the call to worship to set an appropriate stage for worship, but the strength of the choir was also instrumental in supporting the congregation's singing during the opening hymn, and the choir's visible presence filled the chancel.

Unfortunately for the congregation, the choir did not lead worship during the summer. The choir's schedule was entirely appropriate for this church, and I do not intend to be critical, but nonetheless the opening frame of worship suffered as a result of the choir's vacation. In the summer order of worship there was nothing to replace the choral introit. The absence of the choir weakened the congregation's experience of the opening hymn—a situation that only deteriorated if the opening hymn was unfamiliar. There was no formal procession. The chancel seemed empty, and so did the opening frame, which, frankly, had lost a lot of its oomph.

The summer worship frame clearly needed to be strengthened, and it took me a year or two to identify what we could do to bolster it. The change we finally made was a small one. We invited the congregation to stand and sing the first stanza of "Holy, Holy, Holy" immediately after the organ prelude, in place of the choral introit. This addition not only engaged worshipers and added a strong trinitarian bracket to the worship service, but it also evoked the congregation's history: in the early twentieth century "Holy, Holy, Holy" had been the opening hymn the congregation sang every single Sunday, and many members remembered that. This is the same congregation whose signature symbol is its Founders' Day worship service. An evocation of its history and former patterns of worship played to the congregation's strength and sense of identity, so adding a stanza from a favorite hymn to the opening brackets was not disruptive.

I regret to report that I did not take additional steps to strengthen the opening worship frame. I did not even think to address the visual emptiness of the chancel. I made matters worse with my hymn selections; I resisted singing well-loved hymns during the summer, thinking instead that it was a great time to learn new ones. I know now that I made a mistake with those new hymn selections; using more familiar hymns would have strengthened the congregation's singing when summer numbers were down and the choir was absent.

First Presbyterian Church is not unusual in needing to strengthen its summer worship frame. Many other congregations also face this challenge, though undoubtedly the particulars are different. What steps can worship planners and leaders take to make worship frames more robust?

Stop, Listen, and Think

Readers will probably have figured out by now that I am not a big fan of worship change. I thrive on the predictability of worship, and there is nothing I like better than a good, old-fashioned hymn, because I find that I pray most genuinely when I sing hymns. I share this personal information not because I think my preferences should be normative—quite the contrary—but because this background provides the context for my first recommendation about worship change, which is to be cautious. When leaders and congregations consider changes to their worship frames, they will benefit from taking time to slow down, listen to what worshipers have to say, and think about how frames work.

Listen to Worshipers

One of the things I discovered in my research is that church members know a lot about worship. In my conversations with worshipers, I was surprised and humbled by the depth of their understanding and their capacity to articulate the breadth of their knowledge. Even people who were relatively new members and who had grown up outside the church seemed to have a profound understanding of worship.

I began my research by introducing myself to people at coffee hour and asking, "What's good about worship in your church?" My second question was "When you worship, what do you expect and hope for?" As they responded to both questions, people always talked about God. They envisioned God as a willing and eager partner in worship. "God's been waiting for this moment all week, for us to come together and worship and be present with him," one worshiper declared. Another expressed her belief that God tells us to worship: "That's our duty. We are to worship him, and that's what I'm here for, to worship the holy God who so patiently has waited and waited and waited."

These people understood worship as an act of obedience, but at the same time, they experienced it as a blessing. They told me they felt a deep satisfaction when they worshiped, especially if they sensed that they had encountered God. Worship satisfied people if they left it "feeling a little closer," as one person said. Many talked about the benefits of worship, and expressed gratitude for help in dealing with everyday struggles, having a mini-retreat, renewing their energy and focus for the week ahead, or becoming a better person. I was moved by my conversation with a complete stranger, who told me in response to my question that worship had changed his life. "It counters the 'me' orientation," he said, and went on to talk about how much less self-centered he had become as a result of joining the church and worshiping.

I learned much from these conversations. Mostly, I learned to appreciate the deep faith and wisdom that people bring to worship and church life. The worshipers to whom I spoke, whom I selected randomly, knew much more about worship than I thought they would; in retrospect my tendency to underestimate these folks is embarrassing.

I conclude from these conversations that worship leaders like me are not necessarily the congregation's experts on worship. Regular, garden-variety worshipers have a keen understanding of worship, and many have the competence they need to work with their pastors and other leaders to design or tweak worship in their churches. My recommendation is that congregational leaders take time to get acquainted with this local knowledge and use it responsibly in the context of whatever decision-making process works best for the church. Congregational leaders can trust church members to engage in conversations about worship with wisdom and maturity. Worshipers care deeply about worship, and they know what works in their setting.

Consider What Frames Do

When they wish to strengthen worship frames, leaders need also to pause and remember how frames work. Powerful as they are, worship frames are only part of a worship service. Boundary frames play a particular role as worship opens and closes, and mini-frames can highlight certain portions of worship, like sermons or sacraments. Discursive frames found in signature symbols, sermons, and other worship activities can shape and express a congregation's vocation and help members understand how a church interacts with the world around it.

It is also helpful to remember what frames do not do. Although they can shape worship powerfully, frames control neither the movement of the Holy Spirit nor the thoughts and feelings of all worshipers. God and human beings act independently of frames.

Nonetheless, frames have a subtle impact on worshipers, because frames order people's experience in particular ways. Understanding how frames work is knowledge that leaders can use to enhance worship in their congregations.

The boundary frames that comprise the gathering and dismissal phases of worship are important because they define action, focus attention, shape belonging, and sometimes articulate a church's vocation. Every opening frame defines action by ushering worshipers into the physical, emotional, and spiritual space of worship—a space in which they hope somehow to be touched by the grace and wisdom of God. But different worship frames construct this space in various ways, and such differences result in diverse styles of invitation, degrees of formality, emotion norms, and theological emphases. Because worship frames can vary, a congregation needs to know what it believes about worship before it makes any attempts to strengthen worship brackets. To whom does the congregation wish to extend an invitation to worship: its members, newcomers, the unchurched, people of different cultures, or others? What degree of formality best suits the congregation and its worshipers? What emotion norms does the congregation want to establish and follow? What does a congregation want to say about God in worship, how does the church understand its vocation, and how do the current or envisioned frames express these theological convictions?[1] When leaders know what worship frames do in their congregation and what they want them to do better or differently, it will be easier to take whatever steps are appropriate to strengthen worship frames.

Worship frames do more than define action. They also help worshipers pay attention. Responsive and unison participation in the opening frame assists worshipers to get involved in worship; reminders of God's presence, love, and guidance focus worshipers' hearts and minds on their relationship with God; closing brackets help worshipers turn their attention to the world, where they will express their faith in daily living. Wise leaders will consider how their worship frames foster worshipers' concentration, as they ponder how to strengthen worship frames. How do the current opening brackets help worshipers lay aside whatever might distract them, so they can focus on worship? With what styles of participation (silent listening, responsive, unison, etc.) is the congregation involved as worship opens? How does the frame express God's covenant with human beings and help people concentrate on their relationship with God? How does the closing frame express discipleship and focus people's attention on their responsibilities as believers? How will proposed changes support or divert worshipers in their efforts to pay attention? The more aware leaders are of how worship frames function in their worship services, and the clearer leaders are about what they want frames to accomplish, the easier it will be for them to make modifications to strengthen frames.

Worship frames also play a role in shaping a congregation's community, because frame brackets symbolize who belongs in the worshiping assembly and provide opportunities for people to unite their hearts, minds, and voices in the worship of God. Effective gathering phases remind broken, sinful people that God calls and welcomes all—even the most prodigal. Through acts of invitation, expressions of contrition and redemption, and shared participation, frames help a congregation gather its diverse membership into a single worshiping body. Leaders who wish to strengthen the community-building aspects of their worship frames will want to reflect on what their frames say to worshipers and what opportunities they afford for people to unite in worship. Whom does God call the congregation to include in its fellowship, and how does the frame express that explicitly or implicitly? How does the frame express God's love for incomplete, hurting, sinful human beings? Which brackets give people an opportunity to join their voices in song or prayer? How does the combination of worship brackets help people come together into a believing body, a gathered community of faith? Leaders can best strengthen worship frames when they have clarity about the community a congregation feels called to form—its membership and theological convictions—and an understanding of how responsive and unison participation contributes to a church's experience of unity.

In some congregations, opening or closing worship frames express and shape a congregation's vocation. When this is the case, leaders will benefit from coupling their efforts to strengthen a frame with reflection on the church's call. Who are the people of the church, and who are those with and for whom the congregation is called to serve in ministry? What theological convictions shape this church's approach to outreach and fellowship? What programs characterize the congregation's beliefs as it engages the world? When leaders understand the vocational stance of a congregation, they can more easily strengthen worship frames to make them coherent with the church's sense of vocation.

Worship boundary frames are powerful in their capacity to define action, focus attention, shape belonging, and express vocation. They influence how worshipers participate in the service and send subtle messages that shape people's perceptions about a church. Before leaders make changes, it is wise to consider how suggested changes will reshape the frame, send different messages, and affect the congregation.

Strengthening Boundary Frames

Worship leaders can strengthen a boundary frame by changing the opening or closing brackets. The addition of new brackets, the elimination of others, or subtle changes in brackets can alter the overall frame. Frame changes in worship occur frequently throughout the church year, and each change affords leaders an opportunity to make improvements.

In many congregations the shifts to and from summer worship schedules offer the opportunity to strengthen worship frames, since the frames shift anyway. In the example above, the Sunday morning worship frame was changed twice. The summer choir schedule inadvertently weakened the worship frame by eliminating the choral introit, the processional, and the choral presence in the chancel that supported the congregation's worship. It also weakened the closing frame by eliminating the choral amen after the benediction. After a time, we attempted to strengthen the summer worship frame by adding a congregational response at the beginning. We could have done more. In the beginning of worship we could have devised a new processional, used banners or other visual symbols to fill the chancel, or selected hymns that the congregation liked and could sing well (a strategy that would have worked well for this church, although it might backfire at others). In closing brackets we could have added a congregational sung response at the conclusion of worship to replace the choir's regular contribution. More extensive changes might have enhanced the congregation's ability to worship; instead the summer services always seemed a bit flat, because so much was missing. In retrospect, I realize we missed key opportunities to strengthen worship as we shifted from season to season.

Changes in liturgical time also present opportunities to change worship frames. As I discussed earlier, in Advent some churches add an Advent wreath, wreath litany, and Advent hymns as part of the seasonal worship frame. At Christmastime churches display poinsettias or crèches, and sing carols. Easter chancels are awash with lilies and other flowers. Liturgical colors, paraments, banners, other chancel decorations, and vestments change season by season. Liturgical frames change as well with seasonal prayers and responses. Many churches habitually modify worship frames to reflect the changing liturgical seasons, and these changes are so familiar that many worshipers and leaders take them for granted. When done well, such changes can deepen a congregation's worship experience and Christian identity, help it make the shift to a new liturgical season, and highlight the spirit of that season.

Congregational leaders who want to evaluate and possibly strengthen the opening and closing worship frames in their church could think about how frame change occurs throughout the year. Seeing how the congregation is accustomed to shifting frames from one liturgical season to another may suggest additional ways that worship frames can be strengthened within a season. What sorts of visual, sonic, and verbal brackets can be used to enhance a frame's capacity to shape and express action, attention, belonging, or vocation in a congregation? How can a frame be strengthened to help a church worship as authentically and faithfully as possible? Sometimes a change or two in the gathering or dismissal phases can make a big difference.

Mini-Frames

Within a worship service the strategic use of mini-frames can also serve to highlight a particular element of worship. Perhaps a congregation wishes to lift up its sacramental practice and set it apart in a distinctive way. Bracketing strategies that give sharper boundaries to the sacrament can accomplish this. The traditional liturgy for the Sacrament of the Lord's Supper frames the sacrament with a beginning invitation and a concluding prayer of thanksgiving and commitment. This frame can be expanded by adding brackets. Some congregations add a communion hymn or song prior to the invitation, a combination that amplifies God's gracious invitation to table fellowship. The congregation where I worship always recites the twenty-third Psalm (KJV) before the closing communion prayer. Hymns or songs are added to closing communion brackets in other churches. Small additions to a frame like these can be effective, because they help worshipers make transitions in worship and focus people's attention on particular elements of worship.

Not every element of worship needs to be heavily bracketed. Too many smaller frames could be distracting for worshipers. But when smoother transitions are needed, or important dimensions of worship seem to be getting lost, worship leaders may look at that portion of the worship service and consider whether using brackets to frame or reframe that element of worship would strengthen the service.

Strengthening Signature Symbols and Preaching Frames

Many congregations do not have signature symbols that characterize their worship, and others do not enjoy a style of preaching that frames a congregation's vocation. That is perfectly fine, and it's probably appropriate for those congregations. Neither signature symbols nor preaching frames can be forced, nor should they be. In the event, however, that congregations have signature worship symbols or preaching frames, how can they be strengthened?

Some signature symbols are single elements or phases in worship that occur regularly, like Lake View's prayer for peace, House of Hope's worship procession, and the sung response that closes worship at Grace Church. For congregations that practice signature symbols weekly, the symbol could be strengthened in several ways. One strategy would be to use mini-frames to make the symbol more visible. Another approach might be to place the symbol elsewhere in the worship service, and juxtapose it with additional elements of worship that would amplify its message.

The prayer for peace at Lake View, for example, has not always been joined with the opening hymn and expressions of gratitude. When I first witnessed this prayer at the church, it followed the congregation's prayer of confession and an assurance of pardon. Both service placements are appropriate for the prayer for peace, but each also gives it a slightly different cast. When set between the opening hymn and expressions of gratitude, the prayer suggests that through ministries of peacemaking we glorify and thank God. When set side by side with prayers of confession and an assurance of pardon, the prayer couples peacemaking with God's actions of reconciliation in the world. This placement has strong theological logic, but it renders the prayer a bit less visible than it is when it occurs earlier in the service. Altering the placement of a signature symbol in a worship service can modify a frame's message and visibility to some extent.

Annual signature symbols can also be strengthened in various ways. A congregation could make a signature service stand out from other services during the year by using unique bracketing strategies, or bringing in guest choirs or preachers. In addition, fellowship activities or educational programs that accompany the signature symbol service could be reconceived to make the event more festive or meaningful. There are likely dozens of ways that an annual worship service could be set apart to improve the quality of worship or to intensify the framing power of the service itself.

Preaching Frames

How can pastors strengthen preaching frames so that they express a congregation's vocation more clearly or forcefully? To help us consider this question, I turn again to social movement theorists Robert Benford and David Snow, who point out the significance of frames having "resonance" with the people for whom they are constructed. They contend that resonance occurs when frames are consistent with the values and actions of a group, relevant to the group's life and goals, believable because they fit with the group's understanding of the world, and credible because a group trusts the leader who articulates the frame.[2] Ministers can strengthen preaching frames by ensuring that the vocational frames resonate in these ways with their congregations.

Solid preaching frames are consistent and relevant to the life of a congregation. They fit with who a church is, what it does, and what it values. Preachers who want to strengthen the vocational frames they use can do so by ensuring that their words and challenges are consistent with the congregation's practices and vision for itself. This is not to say that a preacher cannot help a congregation stretch itself to try new things or look in new directions, but when she does so, what she says needs to make sense to the church and its history. For example, when John Fry and Jeremiah Wright used preaching frames to help their congregations embrace a new or broader vocation, each did so in ways that affirmed the congregation's values. Fry gave theological grounding to the church's desire to minister faithfully in a community rife with injustice. Wright sought gently to expand a church's commitment to a particular community and its families—a commitment that was already in place. Both honored the congregation's goals and practices in their preaching frames. Ministers can strengthen preaching frames by deepening the consistency or relevancy of the frames, in light of the congregation's understanding of itself, its actions, and its values.

Ministers can also strengthen preaching frames by ensuring their believability. I once heard a preacher tell a story about a sermon he had preached early in his ministry at his new call. In the sermon he had waxed eloquent about the economy. The next week he received a note from a worshiper, along with a subscription to *The Wall Street Journal*. In the note the worshiper stated that he had bought the subscription for the preacher, because he thought that if the preacher was going to talk about the economy, he should at least know what he was talking about.

This preacher is likely not the only person who has stood up in a pulpit and talked at length about something she knew little about. I've certainly made the mistake of relying on surface knowledge about a contemporary issue in sermons. Worshipers, however, are smart and experienced, and most want their preachers to take their knowledge and expertise seriously. When preachers bring in-depth knowledge about the Bible, theology, and contemporary events or situations to the preaching frames they construct, the frames will be more believable, because the frames will reflect the preacher's care and resonate with what some worshipers know already.

Ministers who want to strengthen preaching frames need also to remember to be honest. As Benford and Snow observe, frames resonate when groups trust the people who articulate them. When ministers bring personal, intellectual, and faithful integrity to preaching, it shows. Ministers can strengthen preaching frames by bringing their own deep faith and convictions to the pulpit, and wedding them to the congregation's understanding of its vocation.

Because worship is so different from social movements, I add a final dimension to this discussion of how ministers can strengthen preaching frames, and that is a reminder that we worship for worship's sake and not for any other reason. It is always a temptation to let other priorities intrude into worship, but preachers who want to construct a strong frame will resist that temptation, and let worship focus first and foremost on God, God's embrace of a sinful humanity, and God's will for the world and its people. Truly resonant preaching frames occur only in the context of worship that has integrity.

Why Bother With Frames?

Worship is a fearful and wonderful activity. It is privilege, duty, joy, routine, delight, mystery. It is life-giving to us and our congregations, because it connects us with the God in whom we live and move and have our being. Because it is essential to our lives as people of faith, we work to worship, and we strive to worship well.

Most worship leaders whom I know take seriously the tasks of planning and leading worship, and they are eager to understand as much as they can about how worship works. I have written this book in an attempt to expand our understanding of worship by examining the concept of framing. When I studied and observed worship, it was this sociological concept that helped me best see beneath the surface of different orders of worship and perceive the action that occurred. I discovered interactions and dynamics that have helped me discern how to plan and lead worship more effectively, and I share my learning here, with the hope that you, too, will find framing a useful tool.

I have focused this book on the human and social dynamics of worship structures, and have made practical suggestions for how worship leaders and other church members can employ the concept of framing to understand, plan, and lead worship. Worship frames are powerful. In this book, I have examined how they define action, focus attention, shape community, and articulate a congregation's vocation, and how they can be adapted to support the work of the congregation. The most important aspect of framing in worship, however, is its capacity to help worshipers, leaders, and congregations encounter God and respond faithfully. The power that framing can exert makes it a useful tool for worship leaders to understand and use.

Worship frames, however, are only human instruments in human hands. Although they can be used to support the work of the people as they seek to worship deeply and honestly, they are no substitute for the presence and action of God in worship. In the end, no matter how much effort we expend to shape and direct it, worship is a gift of the Spirit. Some people plan and lead it, and worshipers participate in it, but God enlivens, guides, and receives it. It is my deepest conviction, and I trust it is yours, too, that anybody who thinks seriously about framing worship in a congregation needs to be open to the Holy Spirit's guidance. The good Lord probably has something to say about this, so let us keep our hearts, minds, and ears open.

Questions for Discussion

1. What's good about worship in your church?
2. When you come to worship, what do you hope for and expect?

3. How might you modify worship frames in your church to allow the congregation and its members to worship more faithfully?

Notes

Foreword

1. *Context,* Nov. 15, 2002, from Philip Yancey in *Christianity Today,* Sept. 9, 2002.

2. Quoted by Marva Dawn, *A Royal "Waste" of Time* (Grand Rapids: Eerdmans, 1999), 99.

3. See John Buchanan, *Being Church Becoming Community* (Louisville: Westminster John Knox, 1996), 76.

4. Huston Smith, *Why Religion Matters: The Fate of the Human Spirit in an Age of Disbelief* (New York: HarperOne, 2001), 45.

Preface

1. By traditional worship, I mean the worship practices that have characterized Presbyterians for several decades; this worship style utilizes unison or responsive prayers, and the singing of hymns that are often accompanied by the organ (although some congregations use stringed instruments for accompaniment). By contemporary worship, I mean the worship practices that have been developed by church movements like the Vineyard, Calvary Chapel, and Willow Creek Community Church; this worship style eliminates most unison or responsive prayers, and, rather than hymns, uses praise-and-worship songs accompanied by a praise band (guitars, piano, and sometimes strings, drums, or other instruments). The traditional style is usually more formal than the contemporary. Both incorporate a sermon or message as a central element of worship.

2. Erving Goffman, *Frame Analysis: An Essay on the Organization of Experience* (Boston: Northeastern University Press, 1986; original edition, New York: Harper and Row, 1974), 21. Citations are to the 1986 edition.

Chapter 1

1. In each of these cases, "we" are doctor of ministry classes at McCormick Theological Seminary that I have taught. One of the courses I regularly teach includes participation in worship at these and other congregations.

2. Goffman, *Frame Analysis,* 21.

3. Ronald Heifetz, *Leadership without Easy Answers* (Cambridge: Belknap Press, 1994), 103.

4. See, for example, Donald Capps, *Reframing: A New Method in Pastoral Care* (Minneapolis: Fortress Press, 1990).

5. Goffman, *Frame Analysis,* 251–253.

6. Ibid., chapter 8. By focusing only on his discussion of frame brackets, I have oversimplified Goffman's study of frame analysis, which is remarkably complex and suggestive, and, in fact, provides theoretical background on which the three other approaches build.

7. George Lakoff, *Don't Think of an Elephant! Know Your Values and Frame the Debate* (White River Junction, VT: Chelsea Green Publishing, 2004), xv.

8. Ibid., 3–34, 52–78.

9. Ibid., 3–34, 46–51.

10. See, for example Robert D. Benford and David A. Snow, "Framing Processes and Social Movements: An Overview and Assessment," *Annual Review of Sociology* 26 (2000): 611–39.

11. Heifetz, *Leadership without Easy Answers,* 187.

12. Capps, *Reframing,* 9–51.

13. Lee Bolman and Terrence Deal, *Reframing Organizations: Artistry, Choice, and Leadership* (San Francisco: Jossey-Bass, 1991), 3–19.

14. Nancy Ammerman, Jackson W. Carroll, Carl S. Dudley, and William McKinney, *Studying Congregations: A New Handbook* (Nashville: Abingdon, 1998), 13–16.

15. See, for example, Thomas Hawkins, *The Learning Congregation* (Lousiville: Westminster John Knox, 1997).

Chapter 2

1. Goffman, *Frame Analysis,* 255–56.

2. Norma DeWaal Malefyt and Howard Vanderwell, *Designing Worship Together: Models and Strategies for Worship Planning* (Herndon, VA: Alban Institute, 2005), 145.

3. Goffman, *Frame Analysis*, 256.

4. Thomas G. Long, *Beyond the Worship Wars: Building Vital and Faithful Worship* (Herndon, VA: Alban Institute, 2001).

5. Arnold van Gennep, *The Rites of Passage* (Chicago: University of Chicago Press, 1960 [1909]), 11–25.

6. Ibid.

7. I agree with Michael Ducey, a sociologist and ritual scholar, who notes that Sunday worship in Christian churches is intended not to be a ritual of passage, but rather to interpret everyday life. This insight is reinforced by the testimonies of worshipers and worship leaders, who affirm the importance of worship for interpreting daily life. For a more thorough discussion see Michael Ducey, *Sunday Morning: Aspects of Urban Ritual* (New York: Free Press, 1977), 92.

8. Gennep, *Rites of Passage,* 15–25.

9. Gordon Lathrop, *Holy Things: A Liturgical Theology* (Minneapolis: Fortress Press, 1998), 33–83.

10. Goffman, *Frame Analysis*, chapter 8.

11. I borrow the categories of gathering and dismissal from Malefyt and Vanderwell, 140.

12. Gennep, *Rites of Passage,* 15–17.

13. Malefyt and Vanderwell, *Designing Worship Together*, 140.

14. Goffman, *Frame Analysis,* 252.

15. Hymn text by Fred Pratt Green, copyright © 1979 Hope Publishing Company, Carol Stream, IL 60188. All rights reserved. Used with permission. Reprinted under license #64422.

16. Michael Hawn contrasts community pattern seating with cathedral seating, and I borrow the terms from him. He notes that both pat-

terns have strengths and weaknesses. Michael Hawn, *One Bread, One Body: Exploring Cultural Diversity in Worship* (Herndon, VA: Alban Institute, 2003), 150–51.

17. Gennep, *Rites of Passage*, 12–13, 26–28.

18. Erving Goffman, *The Presentation of Self in Everyday Life* (New York: Anchor Books/Doubleday, 1959), 69.

19. Erving Goffman, *Behavior in Public Places: Notes on the Social Organization of Gatherings* (New York: The Free Press, 1963), 198–216.

20. Deborah Kapp, "The Portrayal of Pastoral Authority in Worship," *Liturgy* 19, no. 4 (2004): 45–56.

21. My understanding of these dynamics is, again, shaped by my reading of Erving Goffman. The insights of Timothy Nelson are also helpful in understanding the emotional dynamics of worship and its leadership. See Goffman, *Behavior*; Erving Goffman, *Interaction Ritual: Essays on Face-to-Face Behavior* (New York: Pantheon, 1967); and Timothy J. Nelson, *Every Time I Feel the Spirit: Religious Experience and Ritual in an African American Church* (New York: New York University Press, 2005). Nelson's work analyzes how emotion is structured throughout worship, not just in the frame.

22. As Nelson notes, "One fundamental difference, then, between 'emotional' and 'nonemotional' worship services is simply the set of rules governing congregational movement and response." Nelson, 151.

23. I define musical genre as a particular type or style of music that is shaped by texts, roots of texts and tunes, emotional orientation, conventions about form and performance, instrumentation, tempo, and means of organizing production and sales. Because they differ in so many of these elements, I argue that hymnody is a distinctly different genre from praise-and-worship music, and that call-and-response music and other songs frequently used in some African American churches are a separate genre, too. See Deborah J. Kapp, "Agency and Authority in the Performance and Practice of Christian Worship: A Study of Worship in Three Presbyterian Congregations" (Ph.D. diss., Loyola University Chicago, 2002), 209–221.

24. Goffman, *Interaction Ritual*, 11–12.

25. Ibid., 35.

26. For an extended discussion of the nature and costs of emotion work, see Arlie Russell Hochschild, *The Managed Heart: Commercialization of Human Feeling* (Berkeley: University of California Press, 1983).

Hochschild studies emotional labor, which she defines as having three characteristics. It requires face-to-face or voice-to-voice contact with the public. It requires the worker to produce an emotional state in others, sometimes at the cost of suppressing one's own feelings and expression. It also allows the employer to exercise a degree of control over the emotional activity of employees. Hochschild, 147.

Chapter 3

1. Robert Glick, *With All Thy Mind: Worship That Honors the Way God Made Us* (Herndon, Va.: Alban Institute, 2006), 133–34.

2. Ibid.

3. Long, *Beyond the Worship Wars*, 47–48, 85–93.

4. Malefyt and Vanderwell, *Designing Worship Together*, 141–42, 173–74.

5. Goffman, *Behavior*, 168.

6. Mihaly Csikszentmihalyi, *Flow: The Psychology of Optimal Experience* (New York: HarperPerennial, 1990), 23–36.

7. Ibid., 211.

8. Ibid., 43–70.

9. Phil Jackson and Hugh Delehanty, *Sacred Hoops: Spiritual Lessons of a Hardwood Warrior* (New York: Hyperion, 1995), 5.

10. Malcolm Gladwell, *The Tipping Point: How Little Things Can Make a Big Difference* (Boston: Back Bay, 2002), 123.

11. I interviewed seventeen people in depth, most for an hour or more, and I conducted a group interview with five men in a men's Bible study. The respondents, who ranged in age from 17 to 70, included men and women who had a range of worship preferences. About half the respondents preferred contemporary worship, and the other half preferred traditional. Worship preferences did not break down along any discernable lines of generation, gender, or church background. Each interview was recorded, transcribed, and analyzed.

12. He told me he found this prayer in *Meditating on the Word* by Dietrich Bonhoeffer.

13. Edward Foley, Capuchin, *Ritual Music: Studies in Liturgical Musicology* (Beltsville, Md.: The Pastoral Press, 1995), 107–113.

14. Foley identifies six musical forms that involve worshipers and leaders to differing degrees: solo, litany, responsory, alternatim, ostinato,

and chorale, Foley, *Ritual Music*, 153–65. Because the litany, responsory, alternatim, and ostinato all involve both leader and worshiper participation, I treat them under the more generic category of "responsive forms."

15. Ibid.

16. Barry Liesch, *The New Worship: Straight Talk on Music and the Church* (Grand Rapids: Baker Books, 1996), 45–69.

17. The musician at St. Luke often selected hymns with texts that are more intimate than that of "Praise, My Soul, the King of Heaven."

18. "Daily Morning Prayer: Rite One," *The Book of Common Prayer and Administration of the Sacraments and Other Rites and Ceremonies of the Church, together with The Psalter or Psalms of David, according to the Use of The Episcopal Church* (New York: Oxford University Press, 1990 [1789]), 37–60.

19. Long, *Beyond the Worship Wars*, 46–48.

20. Hymn text by Carl P. Daw, Jr., copyright © 1990 by Hope Publishing Company, Carol Stream, IL 60148. All rights reserved. Used by permission. Reprinted under license #64422.

21. Hawn, *One Bread, One Body*, 48–49.

22. Joan Huyser-Honig, "The 'In Between' Words: How to Keep Fellow Worshipers Tuned In," *www.calvin.edu/worship/stories/inbetween.php* (accessed January 2, 2008).

23. Stephen Ellingson, *The Megachurch and the Mainline: Remaking Religious Tradition in the Twenty-first Century* (Chicago: University of Chicago Press, 2007), 78–143.

Chapter 4

1. Lathrop, *Holy Things*, 119–32.

2. Sociologists have documented religious mobility and what they call "switching" for several decades. See, for example, Wade Clark Roof and William McKinney, *American Mainline Religion: Its Changing Shape and Future* (New Brunswick: Rutgers University Press, 1987), and Robert Wuthnow, *The Restructuring of American Religion: Society and Faith since World War II* (Princeton: Princeton University Press, 1988).

3. These data are from a small sample—four congregations in a single presbytery. The *identical* membership trajectories are what catch my attention, and suggest an area for further research.

4. Glick offers a helpful summary of the complex challenges that worship leaders face as a result of differences of theology, culture, cognitive style, and generation. Glick, 139–49.

5. Hawn engages the challenges and possibilities of cultural, racial, and ethnic differences in congregational worship. The whole book addresses these challenges; pp. 142–69 include particularly helpful suggestions.

6. Foley, *Ritual Music*, 112.

7. Ibid.

8. Alfred Schutz, "Making Music Together," *Social Research* 18 (March 1951): 76–97.

9. Foley, *Ritual Music*, 165.

10. The Iona Community, *Iona Abbey Worship Book* (Glasgow, U.K.: Wild Goose Publications, 2001), 15–18.

11. Linda Clark, "Hymn-Singing: The Congregation Making Faith," in *Carriers of Faith: Lessons from Congregational Studies*, edited by Carl S. Dudley, Jackson W. Carroll, and James P. Wind (Lousiville: Westminster John Knox, 1991), 51.

12. Hawn, *One Bread, One Body*, 149–50.

13. Ibid., 66.

14. Ibid. 148, 169, 153.

15. Lathrop, *Holy Things*, 210–21.

16. We greeted each other after worship.

17. Lathrop, *Holy Things*, 213.

18. Ibid., 220–21.

19. Ibid., 215–16.

20. Ibid., 174–21.

Chapter 5

1. H. Richard Niebuhr, *Christ and Culture* (New York: Harper and Row, 1951).

2. Jackson W. Carroll, "The Congregation as Chameleon: How the Present Interprets the Past," in *Congregations: Their Power to Form and Transform*, edited by C. Ellis Nelson, 43–69 (Atlanta: John Knox, 1988).

3. Ibid. Carroll does not use the term "vocation," but he does unpack in helpful ways the three tasks of congregational leaders as they stand

on the metaphorical boundary between church and world, and interpret each to the other. Leaders (1) understand and articulate the congregation's identity, (2) understand and articulate what is happening in the world around it, and (3) manage the interface between the two.

4. My understanding of vocation in congregational contexts is shaped by my reading of Calvin, Barth, and the new social-movement theorist Alberto Melucci, who has written extensively on the construction of collective identity in movements. Melucci defines collective identity as the interplay between four variables: intended action, definition of selves and others, field of constraints and opportunities, and meaning of action, which he discusses as ideology. See John Calvin, *Institutes of the Christian Religion*, edited by John T. McNeill, translated by Ford Lewis Battle (Philadelphia: Westminster Press, 1960), 3.10.6; Karl Barth, *Church Dogmatics*, translated by G. W. Bromiley and R. J. Erlich (Edinburgh: T & T Clark, 1962), III. 4. 611–47 and IV. 3. 344; and Alberto Melucci, *Challenging Codes: Collective Action in the Information Age* (Cambridge, U.K.: Cambridge University Press, 1996), 382–91.

5. It may be that the Web is replacing Sunday worship as the initial point of contact for many people who are looking for a church home.

6. As a former staff member (1981–1991) and regular worshiper (1995–present) at Fourth, I know this ministry well. For a fuller examination of Davies's homiletical strategy and the symbolic frame that he constructed for the congregation, see James Wellman, *The Gold Coast Church and the Ghetto: Christ and Culture in Mainline Protestantism* (Urbana and Chicago: University of Illinois Press, 1999), 120–53. Wellman analyzes the ministries of four pastors at Fourth: John Timothy Stone (1909–1929), Harrison Ray Anderson (1929–1962), Davies, and John Buchanan (1985–present). The role of preaching in negotiating cultural change and shaping the symbolic boundaries that define the congregation's vocation is a central theme of the book.

7. Patience and consistency in preaching are crucial if a preacher seeks to establish and nurture a congregation's sense of vocation. Homiletics professor Craig Satterlee points to the importance of patience and sustained preaching messages in congregations that are wrestling with change. See Craig Satterlee, *When God Speaks through Change: Preaching in Times of Congregational Transition* (Herndon, VA: Alban Institute, 2005), 30.

8. On most occasions, Davies steered clear of hot political issues like civil rights or the Vietnam War. He occasionally addressed these but was deliberate in keeping them off the program agenda of the church. He also fostered little interest or programming in overseas mission, believing that Chicago offered more than enough opportunities for outreach and involvement.

9. For a full and careful analysis of how Pfleger framed congregational participation in the marches, see James Cavendish, "To March or Not to March: Clergy Mobilization Strategies and Grassroots Anti-Drug Activism" in *Christian Clergy in American Politics*, edited by Sue E. S. Crawford and Laura R. Olson, pp. 203–26 (Baltimore: Johns Hopkins University Press, 2001).

10. Ibid., 216.

11. Ibid., 204–06.

12. Lakoff, *Don't Think of an Elephant!*, 46–78.

13. Linda J. Clark, Joanne Swenson, and Mark Stamm, *How We Seek God Together: Exploring Worship Style* (Herndon, VA: Alban Institute, 2001).

14. Copies of the congregation's worship bulletins are available on its website: *www.hohchurch.org.*

15. Hawn, *One Bread, One Body*, 48–49.

16. David Roozen, William McKinney, and Jackson Carroll, *Varieties of Religious Presence: Mission in Public Life* (New York: Pilgrim, 1984), 35–36. In this book the authors identify four public stances that characterize congregations: activist, civic, evangelical, and sanctuary. It is from this work that I take the term civic.

17. Clark et al., *How We Seek God Together*, 45–63.

18. Thanks to Carl and Shirley Dudley for pointing out to me the importance of coffee hour in this church.

Chapter 6

1. Goffman, *Frame Analysis,* especially chapters 3, 4, 8, and 12.

2. See ibid., chapter 8, for an extended discussion of bracketing.

3. Lakoff, *Don't Think of an Elephant!.*

4. Heifetz, *Leadership without Easy Answers*, 183–94.

5. One could legitimately argue that this is a very Goffmanesque approach to reframing, and that it more properly fits with a discussion of his theories. Because this approach focuses so heavily on rhetorical approaches and language, and Goffman often put more emphasis on human action than on the content of talk, I address it separately.

6. Capps, *Reframing*, 9–51.

7. Bolman and Deal, *Reframing Organizations*, 320–67.

8. Advent wreath rituals sometimes lack the focus and framing power that they potentially carry. Instead they are sentimental rituals that are not very well anchored in the worship service—nice little add-ons. In congregations where this is the case, perhaps what is needed is a rigorous examination of the worship frame and how its bundle of activities and configurations work together to establish meaningful worship.

9. Chaves, for example, makes this argument. See Mark Chaves, *How Do We Worship?* (Herndon, VA: Alban Institute, 1999), 5.

10. Michael O. Emerson with Rodney M. Woo, *People of the Dream: Multiracial Congregations in the United States* (Princeton: Princeton University Press, 2006), 47–50. Emerson measured charismatic worship with four measures: saying "Amen"; raising hands; spontaneous jumping, shouting, or dancing; and speaking in tongues at least once a year.

11. Ibid., 66–73.

12. Ellingson, *Megachurch and the Mainline*, 107–43.

13. Goffman, *Frame Analysis*, 255.

14. Emerson with Woo, *People of the Dream*.

15. Robert D. Benford and David A. Snow, "Framing Processes," 611–39. Benford and Snow also describe frame bridging, which connects one or more groups of participants around an issue, and frame amplification, which embellishes or clarifies a frame.

16. Ibid.

17. Wright officially retired as senior pastor of Trinity UCC in February 2008. The sermon collection I examine was compiled from sermons that Wright preached in the 1990s.

18. Harold Walker and William Schram, *First Presbyterian Church: Born in the Fort 1833–1983*. Edited by D. Richesin (Chicago: First Presbyterian Church, 1983).

19. Ibid.

20. John R. Fry, *Fire and Blackstone: Non-Sermons by Chicago's White Activist Minister* (Philadelphia: J.P. Lippincott Company, 1969).

21. Ibid., 149–58.

22. Fry's approach and the congregation's ministry were not without their critics. Despite the controversial nature of these ministries, however, Fry's preaching remains a strong example of how homiletical framing can work in situations of change.

23. *www.tucc.org/about.htm* and *www.tucc.org/pastoral_staff.htm* (accessed June 2007).

24. Jeremiah Wright, *Good News! Sermons of Hope for Today's Families* (Valley Forge: Judson, 1995).

25. Ibid., 69.

26. Ibid., 16.

Chapter 7

1. See Malefyt and Vanderwall, *Designing Worship Together*, 71–73, for further discussion of important issues that need to be clarified prior to designing worship.

2. Benford and Snow, "Framing Processes," 619–22.

Suggested Readings

Frame Analysis

Benford, Robert D., and David A. Snow. "Framing Processes and Social Movements: An Overview and Assessment." *Annual Review of Sociology* 26 (2000): 611–39.

For those readers who may be interested in knowing more about framing and social movements, this article is a good place to start, because it reviews the academic conversation. It has a solid bibliography with ample suggestions for additional reading, and the full text is available electronically through academic search engines.

Bolman, Lee, and Terrence Deal. *Reframing Organizations: Artistry, Choice, and Leadership.* San Francisco: Jossey-Bass Publishers, 1991.

Bolman and Deal use frame analysis to help leaders be more imaginative and flexible in the organizations in which they work. The book defines and demonstrates the frames as perspectives approach.

Capps, Donald. *Reframing: A New Method in Pastoral Care.* Minneapolis: Fortress, 1990.

This is a book that pastors will like, because it approaches framing from a church perspective and helps readers to see how framing might be useful in church leadership. Capps uses several approaches to framing, including the problem definition and solution approach.

Goffman, Erving. *Frame Analysis: An Essay on the Organization of Experience.* Boston: Northeastern University Press, 1986 [1974].

You can find in this book almost anything you ever wanted to know about framing but were afraid to ask. Nuanced and comprehensive, this work is the frame "bible" on which much other frame analysis builds—all 550-plus pages of it. Goffman's discussion of bracketing and boundary frames can be found in chapter 8.

Lakoff, George. *Don't Think of an Elephant! Know Your Values and Frame the Debate*. White River Junction, Vt.: Chelsea Green Publishing, 2004.

Lakoff demonstrates how discursive framing works, and attempts to help progressives figure out how to use framing to counter the gains made by political conservatives over the last few decades. Since it is so steeped in contemporary American politics, readers who side with the Democrats may find this more enjoyable than will those who lean toward the Republicans, but whatever one's political persuasion, Lakoff's discussion is precise, readable, and easily understandable.

Worship

Foley, Edward, Capuchin. *Ritual Music: Studies in Liturgical Musicology*. Beltsville, Md.: The Pastoral Press, 1995.

This edited volume pulls together several of Foley's articles about music and worship into a single book. I have used it to help readers see how music gets worshipers involved, but the book raises a host of other interesting ideas, too. Detailed bibliographies identify resources for those who wish to delve further into the role of music in worship.

Hawn, Michael. *One Bread, One Body: Exploring Cultural Diversity in Worship*. Herndon, Va.: Alban Institute, 2003.

This is a very helpful book for readers who want a rich analysis of how to understand and enhance cultural diversity in their congregation and its worship. The book is full of practical suggestions and examples.

Lathrop, Gordon. *Holy Things: A Liturgical Theology*. Minneapolis: Fortress, 1998.

This stimulating book discusses how Christian worship is ordered and the juxtapositional logic that organizes our worship experience. Anyone looking for help in understanding the basic framework of Christian worship will find this book helpful and provocative.

Malefyt, Norma DeWaal, and Howard Vanderwell. *Designing Worship Together: Models and Strategies for Worship Planning.* Herndon, Va.: Alban Institute, 2005.

If your congregation wants to develop or train worship planning teams, this book is a good resource that offers multiple suggestions and examples about how good worship planning occurs.

Congregational Studies and Worship

Readers who enjoy congregational studies might want to read the following books, all of which demonstrate how worship works in particular congregational settings. Each also offers scholarly analysis that allows readers to gain a wider understanding of the social dynamics of worship.

Clark, Linda J., Joanne Swenson, and Mark Stamm. *How We Seek God Together: Exploring Worship Style.* Herndon, VA: Alban Institute, 2001.

I borrowed the idea of signature symbols from this book, which uses the concept to talk about the role of music in expressing and forming a congregation's piety. Based on a study of three congregations, the book discusses signature symbols, church music, and the place of piety in congregational life.

Ellingson, Stephen. *The Megachurch and the Mainline: Remaking Religious Tradition in the Twenty-first Century.* Chicago: University of Chicago Press, 2007.

Ellingson's ethnographic study of nine Lutheran churches in the Pacific Northwest is a fascinating analysis of how megachurch models and successes influence smaller congregations, some of which try to adopt megachurch approaches in their settings. The book discusses worship practices extensively and, among other things, examines how worship shapes a congregation's theology.

Emerson, Michael O., with Rodney M. Woo. *People of the Dream: Multiracial Congregations in the United States.* Princeton, N.J.: Princeton University Press, 2006.

This book is one of several resources to emerge from a larger project that Emerson and others are conducting about multiracial churches in the United States. I found this work particularly useful because it provides an in-depth study of how one congregation changed its practices (including worship) to expand its diversity and outreach. The book includes concrete suggestions and is forthright about the joys and challenges of trying to expand a congregation's diversity.

Nelson, Timothy. *Every Time I Feel the Spirit: Religious Experience and Ritual in an African American Church*. New York: New York University Press, 2005.

This study of worship in a Pentecostal church in South Carolina is very good. I loved it, and I was helped especially by Nelson's extensive analysis of how emotion is structured in worship.

Preaching and Congregational Leadership

None of the resources cited below uses the language of "congregational vocation" or "frame" in the ways that I do, yet these document how preachers can use preaching frames to articulate their churches' calls to mission and service in their communities.

Cavendish, James. "To March or Not to March: Clergy Mobilization Strategies and Grassroots Anti-Drug Activism." In *Christian Clergy in American Politics*, edited by Sue E. S. Crawford and Laura R. Olson. Baltimore: Johns Hopkins University Press, 2001.

Cavendish details how the preaching of the Rev. Michael Pfleger constructed a preaching frame that articulated the church's call to serve and transform its community, and effectively mobilized congregants to be involved in anti-drug marches.

Nieman, James R. *Knowing the Context: Frames, Tools and Signs for Preaching*. Minneapolis: Fortress, 2008.

This book uses the concept of framing to help ministers better exegete their contexts and preach cross-culturally.

Wellman, James K. *The Gold Coast Church and the Ghetto: Christ and Culture in Mainline Protestantism*. Urbana and Chicago: University of Illinois Press, 1999.

Wellman analyzes the ministry of the four pastors of Fourth Presbyterian Church in Chicago, from 1909 to the present, in light of the cultural changes they negotiated. The book demonstrates how these pastors used preaching and other leadership efforts to help their congregation adapt to cultural change.

Sermon Collections

Fry, John R. *Fire and Blackstone: Non-Sermons by Chicago's White Activist Minister.* Philadelphia: J. P. Lippincott, 1969.

Fry's sermons are interspersed with essays that describe the changes and challenges in the immediate neighborhood that compelled the church to seek a new vocation. The sermons are imaginative, lively, and bold.

Wright, Jeremiah. *Good News! Sermons of Hope for Today's Families.* Valley Forge, Pa.: Judson, 1995.

Brief introductory texts in this collection place the sermons in context. These are strong, biblical sermons that will enrich any reader.